A Collection of 4 Best-Selling Books

PRICE
of SPIRITUAL
POWER

ROBERTS LIARDON

Banner
Publishing

THE PRICE OF SPIRITUAL POWER:
A Collection of Four Bestsellers in One Volume

Books Included:
Holding to the Word of the Lord
The Quest for Spiritual Hunger
The Price of Spiritual Hunger
Spiritual Timing

Roberts Liardon Ministries
P.O. Box 2989
Sarasota, FL 34230
E-mail: info1@robertsliardon.org
www.RobertsLiardon.com

ISBN: 978-1-62911-221-3
eBook ISBN: 978-1-62911-222-0
Printed in the United States of America
© 2014 by Roberts Liardon

Banner Publishing
1030 Hunt Valley Circle
New Kensington, PA 15068

1 2 3 4 5 6 7 8 9 10 11 ⊵ 21 20 19 18 17 16 15 14

CONTENTS

HOLDING TO THE WORD OF THE LORD

By Roberts Liardon

CONTENTS

1

WHEN LOGIC AND FAITH COLLIDE

Picture this: You're sitting in a boat, far out on a lake and miles away from the nearest shore. Suddenly, you hear the unmistakable voice of God: "Get out of the boat and walk on the water."

What would you do?

First of all, you would probably bang yourself on the side of the head a couple of times to make sure you weren't hearing things. But suppose that even after you did that, the voice still came as consistent and as loud as ever before.

"Get out of the boat and walk on the water."

There would be only one thing to do in a situation like that—get out of the boat and start walking on the water, as God's voice instructed you to do.

That's what happened to the apostle Peter. When he stepped out of the boat, it was, to anyone else who may have been watching, a very illogical and perhaps even silly thing to do. But as long as Peter was responding in faith, the water might as well have been solid ground because it supported his body without a bit of trouble. However, as soon as Peter took his eyes off Jesus and looked at what he was doing from a logical perspective, he was in big trouble. He began to sink as if he was wearing concrete boots.

I don't think it's likely that God is going to tell you to go walking across the nearest lake, but then again, He might. Whatever

He calls you to do, there are bound to be times when His direct word to you will collide with the world's notion of logic and good sense. (By "word" I mean His prophetic word as compared to God's "Word" in the Bible.) Other people will tell you that you're foolish if you follow the Lord. Your own brain may tell you that you're foolish if you follow after a word the Lord has given to you. But you're never foolish to hold to God's word. Never in a billion years can you make a wrong move by doing what He tells you to do.

The truth is, when "logic" collides with a direct word from God, logic crumbles into little pieces while the word remains unbroken and unmoved.

The Bible is full of examples of people who were willing to follow God's word instead of logic and were blessed beyond measure because of it. For example, it was not logical for a humble shepherd named Moses to go before the mighty Pharaoh and demand that the children of Israel be set free, but that's what God told Moses to do, and that's what he did. Because of it, the Israelites were able to leave Egypt and make their way to the Promised Land. (See Exodus 3–12.)

It wasn't logical for Noah to build a huge boat so far from the nearest ocean, but he was obeying God when he did it, and as a result, only Noah and his family survived a worldwide calamity. (See Genesis 6–9.)

It wasn't logical for Gideon to go up against the entire fury of the Midianite army with a tiny group of men who armed themselves with nothing more than pitchers and trumpets, but he did what the word of the Lord commanded, and as a result, the nation of Israel threw off its oppressors and gained its independence. (See Judges 6:12–7:25.)

Nor was it logical for Abraham to believe it when God pronounced him to be the father of many nations. After all, he didn't have any children, and he and his wife, Sarah, were well past the age of childbearing. Abraham could have looked at himself, shook his head, and said, "Lord, You must have me mixed up with someone else." But he didn't, and Abraham did indeed become the father of many nations, just as God had promised he would. (See Genesis 17:4.) It was through the lineage of Abraham that Jesus Christ came into the world in the flesh, so all of us who have surrendered our lives to Christ can consider ourselves to be sons and daughters of Abraham. (See Matthew 1:17.)

Abraham is a great example of someone who believed God's word in spite of what his natural mind told him. Romans 4:3 tells us that *"Abraham believed God, and it was accounted unto him for righteousness."*

> *Therefore it is of faith, that it might be by grace; to the end the promise might be sure to all the seed; not to that only which is of the law, but to that also which is of the faith of Abraham; who is the father of us all, (as it is written, I have made thee a father of many nations,) before him whom he believed, even God, who quickeneth the dead, and calleth those things which be not as though they were. Who against hope believed in hope, that he might become the father of many nations, according to that which was spoken, So shall thy seed be. And being not weak in faith, he considered not his own body now dead, when he was about an hundred years old, neither yet the deadness of Sarah's womb: He staggered not at the promise of God through unbelief but was strong in faith, giving glory to God; and being fully persuaded that what he had promised, he was also able to perform.*   (Romans 4:16–21)

God may be speaking to you about something the same way He spoke to Abraham, but you're struggling to trust God's Word in the midst of the reality you see all around you. I have seen and experienced the same struggles that many people go through.

For example, when I was still a young boy, the Lord told me that He was going to send me to the nations to preach for Him. My logical mind said, *What's this about going around the world for God? You don't even have a car! And even if you did, you couldn't afford enough gas to get to the other side of town—much less go to the other side of the world.*

In spite of the doubts that assailed me, I clung fast to the word the Lord had spoken. I got a map of the world, put it on my wall, and every morning when I got up to get ready for school, I would hit that map and say, "I'm coming to you—open up!" I kept saying that day after day, even though some days my head would tell me I was crazy. And you know what? God has taken me to more than sixty countries throughout the world to proclaim salvation through Jesus Christ!

At first, it wasn't easy for me to get used to doing so much traveling. If I had my own way, I would rather have stayed home where I was comfortable. Traveling can be very hard on the human body, especially when you're always going back and forth across time zones and experiencing jet lag. Sometimes you can't remember what day it is, much less what time it is. It seems like you're always standing in lines, looking for your luggage, and trying to get used to the local food and the local customs. I was always so glad when I returned home to the United States where I could drink the water right out of the tap without worrying about getting sick and where I could flip a switch and have electric lights any time of the day or night.

Although the traveling was often exhausting, I loved having a chance to see people in other countries and to tell them about Jesus. After a while, the traveling wasn't so bad as I began to see the harvests come in from the seeds I had planted. For another thing, the desire to preach the Gospel was so strong in me that if I wasn't out on the road, I would begin to feel antsy and unfulfilled—as if I really wasn't doing what God had called me to do.

And then He spoke to me again. "Roberts, I want you to build a school for My glory."

But Lord, my mind protested, *I'm spending so much time on the road. How in the world could I ever build a school for You?*

But the Lord's voice was persistent, and I knew I would obey—had to obey. As He commanded, I would build a Bible school where young men and women would be taught how to be effective ministers of the Gospel. It meant an entirely new direction for me. It meant that I couldn't travel as much. It felt strange at first, but then came the peaceful assurance that always accompanies obedience.

Has God spoken a specific thing for you to do? Perhaps He has given you something that may not even be in the same ballpark with what you are doing right now. You might even be scratching your head and saying, "Well, I sure don't see how that's going to happen." But you don't have to see how it's going to happen. You just have to trust the Lord, know that His Word is always true, and what He has proclaimed for you *will* come to pass if you are obedient and yielded to Him.

Another thing to keep in mind is that you cannot dictate to God how things are going to work out. You can't tell him, "Well, God, this is how I want You to do it." You must be yielded to Him.

God is not a cosmic errand boy who jumps when we call His name, but He is a loving Father who wants only the best for us. He can mold us into what He wants us to be. It's truly amazing what God can do in the lives of those who really believe His Word.

One year I held a big convention in Minneapolis, Minnesota. At the beginning, I was really worried, because we had so many big-name speakers coming in and our expenses were going to run more than $100,000 for the week. I don't know about you, but that's a lot of money for me. I kept thinking, *What if no one comes? What are we going to do if we can't pay our bilk? What if I'm being presumptuous or foolish?* That was fear rising up within me because I knew in my spirit that I was doing exactly what God had told me to do. Deep down inside of me, I knew there wouldn't be any problem in paying the bills and blessing the ministries of the speakers who had been asked to participate in the convention, but I really had to cling to the sword of the Lord in that regard because the soul and the flesh were fighting against my faith.

Every time I go somewhere to preach a series of messages or conduct a seminar or a convention, my natural mind always says to me, *What if no one comes?* And then, when the meetings start and the people come, I always look around and think, *Wow! Just look at all these people! They really came!*

I have to get hold of myself, shake myself a little bit, and remind myself that I am doing what God has asked me to do. I serve the most awesome, powerful God. He spoke this entire universe into existence! You just can't go wrong when you're following Him.

Several years ago, I read a true story written by the mother of a little boy who was in the third grade. This mom was listening to her son say his prayers one night and was shocked to hear him say, "And thank You, Lord, that You're going to let me fly."

When the mother questioned her little boy about his prayer, he said he was certain that God had spoken to him and told him that he was going to be able to fly.

"You mean on a big airplane, like when we go to see your grandpa?"

"No, like this." And the little guy began flapping his arms like a bird.

Naturally, the mother didn't know what to do. After all, she knew little boys can't fly by flapping their arms. But she had worked so hard to build up her son's faith, she didn't want to do or say anything that might damage it. In the weeks that followed, he kept believing that he was going to be able to flap his wings and fly around the room. His faith never wavered. Then one day, the little boy came home from school all excited. It seemed his class was going to put on a performance of Peter Pan, and he had been selected for the starring role!

When the day of the performance came, the mother and the little boy saw God's word fulfilled. The school had rigged up a contraption consisting of ropes and pulleys whereby Peter Pan was able to "fly" around the room. The little boy was absolutely beside himself with delight. As soon as the performance was over, he ran into his mother's arms and said, "See? I told you God said He was going to let me fly!"

Now you may be thinking that it's a very long way from that fulfillment of God's word to the little boy to the fulfillment of what He has spoken to you. But, is it really? A little boy believed that God would let him fly around the room and he did fly around the room. Perhaps God has been calling you to do something great for His kingdom, and you look around yourself and say, "How, Lord? I can't do something like that." Oh, yes, you can. If you accept and believe God's word to you with the faith of a child, you will see the glory of the Lord in your life!

> Verily I say unto you, Except ye be converted, and become as little children, ye shall not enter into the kingdom of heaven.
> (Matthew 18:3)

What did Abraham do when God spoke to him? He began to speak the same language God was speaking. Abraham agreed with

God that what He had said was true, "Yes, Lord, I believe that I will be the father of many nations."

When God speaks to you, your language must begin to echo God's language. When Abraham first began to say, "I am the father of many nations," I'm sure his friends and neighbors must have thought he was totally out of his mind. Can't you picture them pointing at him and laughing behind his back? "Poor old guy has really lost his mind. He doesn't even have one child, and he thinks he's the father of many nations." Abraham let them laugh. He didn't know how the word of the Lord was going to be fulfilled, but he knew it was going to happen.

Plenty of people in this world like nothing better than to run around popping other people's balloons. They don't want God's word to come true. They don't want you to succeed. But don't listen to them. Listen to God!

It's easy to hold on to a word from the Lord when everyone around you agrees with it. It's not so easy when they are vehement in their opposition to it.

When I was still in my teens, God called me into the ministry. He wasn't telling me that He wanted me to go into the ministry *someday*. He was telling me that He wanted me to start preaching *right now*.

Not everybody was thrilled with the idea of a boy-preacher. I heard comments like, "You're too young to be a preacher," and "Are you sure you're really listening to God?" Some people thought I was being presumptuous or was getting carried away with a sense of my own importance. They wanted me to know my place and stay there—to do the things "normal" teenagers do.

But it didn't matter to me what anyone else said. Even at that early age, I knew that God's voice was the only one really worth listening to. I began preaching in churches throughout my hometown of Tulsa, Oklahoma, and as a result of my obedience to God's word, I saw hundreds of people come to salvation through faith in Jesus Christ.

Unfortunately, this world of ours is full of critics. Do you know what a critic is? A critic is someone who can't or won't try to do anything himself but gets great delight out of criticizing others who do try to do things.

The critic says, "This guy's not much of a teacher," but they won't volunteer to teach. The critic says, "Can you believe she had the nerve to sing a solo in church with her voice?" But they're not about to get up and use their own voice to glorify God. The critic says, "This fellow's got a lot of nerve, thinking that God has told him to start a Bible school." But they don't take the time to listen to what God might be saying to them.

Some people see the negative in every situation. We give them some good news and they quickly respond with, "Yes, but." That's their favorite saying, "Yes, but." "Yes, but what about this?" "Yes, but have you thought about that?" "Yes, but what if such-and-such happens?" Sometimes I have just had to look someone like that right in the eye and say, "Oh, shut up, in Jesus' name!"

I was so happy and excited when God spoke to me that I could scarcely contain my joy, but then some of my friends started saying, "Well, Roberts, what about this or that?" Their arguments were terribly disappointing because I didn't ask for a dissecting of the word from the Lord. I wanted my friends to be excited with me regarding what God was going to be doing in my life!

Abraham didn't ask God to give him two chapters of explanation on how it was going to be possible for him and Sarah to have a child at their advanced age. He just believed God and agreed that he would father many nations. Abraham didn't look at Sarah and say, "No way!" Sarah didn't look at him and say, "That's right.

No way!" Abraham and Sarah held fast to what God had said to them.

> He staggered not at the promise of God through unbelief; but was strong in faith, giving glory to God; and being fully persuaded, that what he had promised, he was able also to perform.   (Romans 4:20–21)

What does it mean to be *fully persuaded*? I like what Oral Roberts says, "It means that you know that you know that you know that you know, that you know that you know that you know that you know, that you know that you know it's so." And that's the way it was for Abraham. If you find yourself surrounded by critics and naysayers, you have to keep in mind that if God has told you to do something, He knows you have the ability and the resources to do it. You can be assured that He will work through you to accomplish His purpose in your life.

Are people criticizing you and saying negative things about you because you are holding fast to God's Word? Read on to find out what critics have said about some other familiar people.

Early in her career, a movie producer told Lucille Ball that she had absolutely no acting talent and she ought to forget about being in show business. She didn't listen, and all of us who have laughed at her antics are very glad she didn't.

A publishing company sent a letter to a beginning author by the name of Zane Grey saying that he couldn't write, would never be able to write, and that they wished he would stop wasting their time with his material. But Grey kept on writing and wound up with literally dozens of best-sellers and has sold millions of books.

Thomas Edison's father believed his son to be a "dunce," and once whipped the boy in public for his failures at school. When Ludwig van Beethoven was a boy, his piano teacher pronounced him as being "hopeless" and said he had no musical ability whatsoever. I could go on with page after page of examples of people who refused to listen to their critics, and instead, continued to pursue their dreams. I am not saying that all of the people I have listed were particularly godly or that they were following what God had told them to do. I don't know about that one way or the other. But I do know that they didn't listen to their critics and neither should you—especially when God is on your side!

Faith cometh by hearing, and hearing by the word of God.
(Romans 10:17)

Listen to God's word to you rather than the words of the critics and the naysayers, and your faith will be built up to the point where you can see past the barriers and the obstacles that might otherwise keep you from finishing the work to which God has called you.

Faith causes things to happen. Abraham was not weak in faith. He kept rehearsing what God had said and kept on holding on to it. He could have focused on the negatives: "I'm an old man. Sarah is an old woman. We've been married all these years without having any children, so how in the world can I believe I'm going to have a son now?" Instead, Abraham stayed focused on God's Word to him: "You will be the father of many nations."

I am surprised at how many people in the modern world try to tell God what to think and how to act. Our society is full of people trying to act like Jehovah. When you begin to obey, that's when they start to criticize. "Well, I just don't think you ought to do that." Those people need to think less and believe and obey more. The Bible says that Abraham held to faith, not being weak in faith. He built himself up. *"He considered not his own body now dead"* (Romans 4:19). He lived in faith that what God had said to him would come to pass, no matter how impossible it may have looked to those who were seeing only through physical eyes.

Always remember that your security is in the Word of God. There is no security in how much money you have, what kind of car you drive, or how fancy your home is. There is no security in your career or the investments you make. There is not even any security in the relationships you have with other people. Your money may be stolen, your house may burn down, you may lose your job, and your investments may go sour. Even your friends and loved ones may disappoint you. Security is found in only one place in this world and that is in the abiding Word of God.

I don't mean to imply that God's Word won't be challenging. It may shake you out of your routine or rock your comfort zone. But it is true that following and obeying His Word is the only possible source of lasting security.

Some in the charismatic movement have gotten to the point where they believe that God only speaks to us with nice, sweet little encouraging words. He says things like, "Oh, My people, I love you. Hang in there and everything will be all right. I know life can be hard sometimes, but remember that I love you; and it will help you get through."

I'm not doubting God's love for a moment, and I do believe that He wants us all to be encouraged and strengthened by His presence in our lives. But I know that He is also calling us to boldness and action on His behalf.

He may tell you something like, "I want you to build a big church for me."

"Who, me?" you respond with surprise. Yes, you.

"Oh...uh ...well, I thought God was talking to me, but it must have been the devil. After all, God only says things like, 'Be encouraged. Be at peace. I love you.'"

The God we serve is not like that. He often says things like, "I want you to go into other nations and preach the gospel." "I want you to feed the poor in My name." "I want you to get involved in a crisis pregnancy center where you can help save lives." "I want you to become a missionary."

But some of us answer, "What? Me? Oh, well, listen Lord, You must not know me very well. I can't start a church for You! Why, I can hardly pay my light bill. My children are in rebellion. My life is so mixed up and confused. Please don't ask me to do something great for You!"

Well, let me tell you, if God didn't see in you the ability and capacity to do great things for Him, He wouldn't ask you to do those things. He knows the greatness He has built into you, and He wants to work with and through you to develop and utilize it.

What is God saying to you? Whatever His word is to you, believe it, act upon it, and just watch what happens!

2

DON'T EVER LET GO—
EVEN IN A VICTORY

When the apostle Peter began walking on the water, he soon became distracted by the wind and the waves, momentarily lost his faith, and began to sink like a rock. That moment was undoubtedly etched in Peter's mind forever as one of his biggest failures. But actually, it began one of his greatest successes. Peter was doing what no other man has ever done, with the exception of Jesus. He was walking along on the Sea of Galilee like someone out for a Sunday afternoon stroll. Imagine how the apostles felt when they saw Peter get out of that boat and start walking on the water.

"Look at him, he's actually walking on the water! Can you believe it?"

I'm sure their brother's demonstration of faith thrilled and amazed them, but that's not where the story ended. In his moment of victory, Peter let go of God's word, and his moment of failure swallowed up his triumph. I have seen that sort of thing happen so many times. Sometimes people let go of God's word because the success that has come their way surprises them. They think, like Peter did, *I can't really be doing this! Something's bound to go wrong. I just know it's all going to fall apart.* And when their fears become stronger than their faith, it does fall apart.

Other people have let go of God's word because they have become overly confident. They've built up some kind of personal empire that seems to be running well, and they get to the point where they no longer think they need to listen to God. God may even be telling them that it's time to move on in an entirely new direction, but they're not listening. Instead, they're doing the same old thing, only now they're trying to do it in their own power instead of in God's power, and that always means disaster.

Some people tend to look at God in the same way a child would look at a parent who was teaching him how to ride a bicycle. Dad's running along behind his little boy who's trying his best to keep the handlebars steady and pedal at the same time. Finally, Dad gives a big push and the youngster is riding on his own. "Thanks, Dad, but I don't need your help anymore!" the boy yells as he pedals down the street.

We can never say, "Thanks, God, but we don't need Your help anymore." We always need His help! As long as you and I are living on this planet, we are going to face challenges and hurdles. Satan will never stop trying to cause us to stumble, so there's never a time when it's okay to let go of God's Word or His hand.

Sometimes the Lord may tell you to do something that seems totally contradictory to everything else He has asked you to do. If this is the case, there are a couple of things to keep in mind. The first is that the Lord is the only One who knows how things are going to come together in your life. He is the only One who sees the twists and turns that will be necessary to get you to where you need to be—to where He wants you to be. The second thing is that God may be wanting to purify your motives. In other words, He wants to ensure that you are holding to His word because you believe and trust Him no matter what and not because you are only looking for the things He can give you.

To explain what I'm talking about, let's take a look at Abraham and Isaac. We've already talked about how Abraham believed God's promise that he would become the father of many nations, even though he and his wife were both old and had no children. And so, true to the word of the Lord, Sarah conceived and gave birth to Isaac.

I hope that when Isaac was born, Abraham and Sarah threw a huge party to celebrate, and I hope they invited all of the people who earlier had said, "Abraham, you're crazy to go around saying God told you that you would be the father of many nations. You must be delirious. God hasn't spoken to you."

I'm sure it would have given Abraham a great deal of satisfaction to show off his baby boy and say things like, "Would you like to hold my delusion for a while? Hey, you who ridiculed me the most, how would you like to change his diapers?" How good it must have been for Abraham to be able to say, "See what God can do! He is always true to His word!"

And then what happened? God said, "Abraham, I want you to go out into the wilderness to offer me a sacrifice—your son, Isaac."

Imagine how Abraham must have felt when he heard those words. He had waited so long for this little boy to be born. He had held on to God's promise that he would become the father of many nations, even when his friends and neighbors laughed at him. And now, as a very old man, he was experiencing for the very first time the joy of a developing father-son relationship. He was discovering what a wonderful feeling parental love can be.

God said, "I want you to show Me how much you love Me by giving Me the life of your only son."

What would you have done if you were Abraham? Most of us would probably have thrown what my mother used to call a "conniption fit."

"What are You talking about, Lord? How can You ask me to do something like this? All of my friends thought I was a nut for believing You when You said I was going to be a father, and now they're really going to think I'm a nut if I offer my only son as a sacrifice. I just can't do it! I *won't* do it!"

You see, Abraham had attained his goal. He had become a father. But then came the next challenge—a test to see whether he was willing to sacrifice everything in order to obey God.

> *By faith Abraham, when he was tried, offered up Isaac: and he that had received the promises offered up his only begotten son, of whom it was said, That in Isaac shall thy seed be called: accounting that God was able to raise him up, even from the dead; from whence also he received him in a figure.*
> (Hebrews 11:17–19)

Abraham walked out of his home that morning on his way to offer a sacrifice to the Lord. His servants were with him, Isaac was with him, but there wasn't anything else for a sacrifice—no ram, goat, or bull. Picture little Isaac running on ahead of everyone, doing the things little boys do—throwing rocks, kicking at sticks and leaves, and asking a hundred questions, such as, "Dad, what are we going to sacrifice?"

Abraham answers softly, "It's okay, son. We'll find something to sacrifice. God will provide." Yet, he knows all the while that his precious little boy is going to be placed upon that altar.

He would not be dissuaded from holding fast to the word of the Lord, nor from his faith that God always knows what was right and best. If God said, "I want you to give me your son," then Abraham was going to give God his son. It was that simple.

And so this little procession arrives at the spot where the sacrifice is to take place. Abraham piles the wood on top of the altar and makes other preparations for the sacrifice, and little Isaac is looking around, more perplexed than ever: "I don't understand, Dad. We don't have any animals with us."

And Abraham is forced to say, "My son, you are the sacrifice." Having said that, Abraham ties the little boy up, places him on the altar, and prepares to strike him dead. But it is precisely at that moment, and not a moment sooner, that an angel stops Abraham and tells him that God does not want him to offer the boy as a sacrifice but was only testing his faithfulness.

Now Abraham didn't know that was going to happen. When he raised his knife to strike his son, he didn't understand why this was what God commanded, but he was willing to do it anyway. And he was still believing God's promise that he would be the father of many nations. In the natural, there was no way for Abraham to fit all the pieces together. They just did not make sense. Abraham was willing to say, "Lord, I don't understand it, but You do. And I can't do anything other than trust You."

You see, similar things will happen in your life as you face challenges and oppositions. It will look like if you do the things God is telling you to do that everything will be destroyed instead of built up. Persecutions and accusations will come along designed to make you withdraw from the word the Lord has given you and to keep you from being strong in the faith. You will be hit in your spirit, tempting you to let go of the word and hold on to natural things. But if you let go of God's word to you, you will die!

I have held on to what God has said to me and have not let go of it. I've been hit and I've had victories. I have learned that whatever seems to be happening, whether it is good or bad, the most important thing I can do is to hold on to God s Word. It is my foundation and it is my security!

"Roberts, do you know what you're doing?" "Yes, I'm doing what God has told me to do."

"But do you understand what the outcome of this will be?"

"No, I don't need to understand that. All I need to know is that God told me to do it, and He expects me to obey."

Don't Question, Just Obey!

Obedience, and not our own understanding, is the key. It's not important for me to understand *why* God wants me to do something. It is important for me to know *what* He is telling me to do and to be willing to do it. As we can see from the life of Abraham, it is not always easy to hold fast to the word of the Lord. It can be terribly, terribly difficult. In fact, the Bible has many accounts of people who tried to run away from God's word, but who ultimately found their destinies in obedience.

For example, Moses didn't want to obey when God told him that he had been chosen to bring the children of Israel out of Egypt. He said something like this: "But Lord, you know how tongue-tied I get. I'll get in front of Pharaoh and start stammering and stuttering and make a complete fool of myself. I really don't think that will convince him that I'm a representative of the One who created the universe." (See Exodus 4:10.) But eventually, Moses agreed to do things God's way, and he became the great leader of an entire nation.

When the word of God came to a young man named Saul, telling him that he had been chosen to be the first king of Israel, Saul tried to hide among some baggage. (See 1 Samuel 10:21–22.) He must have been thinking something like, *What? Me, a king? God, You must have me mixed up with someone else. I don't want the job. Please, I'm not qualified!* But God would not be dissuaded from His choice of Saul, and he went on to lead Israel into a number of great military victories. (See 1 Samuel 14:47–48.)

When God told Gideon that he had been chosen to lead the Israelites into battle against their oppressors, the Midianites, Gideon replied that he couldn't do it because he came from the least of the families of Israel and he was the least one in that least family. But God knew who He was choosing, and Gideon went on to prove on the battlefield that God's choice was the correct one. (See Judges 6–8.)

There are other examples. Jonah tried to run in the opposite direction when God told him to go preach repentance to the people who lived in Nineveh. (See Jonah 1:1-3.) Jeremiah told God he couldn't speak to the people because he was only a youth. (See Jeremiah 1:6.) Elijah fled into the wilderness and hid because he thought he was the only one left who was on God's side. (See 1 Kings 19:14.)

Take a closer look at the lives of some of these heroes from the Bible, and you'll find out that they stumbled not at the beginning of their walk with the Lord, but much later on when they had gained a bit more confidence and when they were flush with the heady feeling of success.

For example, it wasn't until Moses struck a rock to get water for the people, instead of speaking to the rock as God had commanded him to do, that he got into trouble. It seemed natural to Moses to strike the rock because he had done it so many times before. But this time, God had clearly said to speak to the rock and the water would pour forth. Moses wasn't listening, and he did the wrong thing. As a result, he was not allowed to enter the Promised Land. (See Numbers 20:8–12.)

The same thing happened with Saul. God ordered him to destroy all of the Amalekites, but he didn't listen, and as a result the kingdom was taken away from him and given to David. (See 1 Samuel 15:1–29.)

And look at Gideon. Fresh from his victory on the battlefield, Gideon fashioned an idol which became a snare to Gideon and to his house. (See Judges 8:22–28.)

Note that it wasn't in the beginning that these people stumbled; it was when they were gaining confidence. They were feeling pretty good about themselves. Perhaps they thought they didn't need to listen all that closely to the word of the Lord anymore.

I don't know of anyone who doesn't need to listen to the word of the Lord. There are a lot of people who aren't listening to what God has to say, and that's why the world is in such a mess. Remember the old commercial that said, "When E. F. Hutton speaks, everyone listens"? Wouldn't this world of ours be a wonderful place if it were true that when God spoke, everyone listened? It's not going to happen this side of the millennium, but it can happen on a personal level in your life. There is peace, prosperity, and joy in following the word of the Lord.

> Man does not live on bread alone but on every word that comes from the mouth of the LORD.
> (Deuteronomy 8:3 NIV)

Make a decision that from this day on, you will hold tightly to God's word for you. This is a decision you will never regret!

3

WHY YOU DON'T NEED A "PLAN B"

Let's take one more look at Peter sitting in the boat on the Sea of Galilee. He looks up and sees Jesus walking toward him, coming right over the top of the water.

"Lord," he says, "if it's You, let me get out of the boat and walk to You."

And Jesus replies simply, "Come."

Peter immediately climbed out of the boat and started walking on the water, heading toward Jesus. Admittedly, he didn't get very far. The Bible tells us that this event took place on a very windy night, that the wind and the waves took Peter's attention away from his Lord and caused him to begin to sink. But what ended up as a rather spectacular failure started out to be a spectacular triumph of faith. For a while, Peter was dancing over those waves like there was nothing to it.

I admire Peter for having the faith and the courage to get out of the boat in the first place. I also admire him for the speed with which he followed his Lord's command to "come." Peter didn't spend a moment trying to put together an alternative plan. He didn't say, "Er ... okay, Lord, I'll be right there. But just in case it doesn't work, let me look around here and see if I can find a flotation device." He didn't even turn to the other disciples and say, "Okay, guys, I'm going to get out of this boat and try to walk on the water. But if it doesn't work, I want you all to be ready to haul me back in."

No, Peter got out of that boat and started walking across the water. I believe that far too many people today are only halfhearted in their obedience to the word of God. They say, "Okay Lord, I hear You and I'm willing to follow. But just the same, I think I better have a couple of alternatives in mind in the event that what You have planned for me doesn't work out." Such thinking shows a complete lack of understanding of the power and faithfulness of God. It can only lead to trouble.

Plan B Always Leads to Trouble

Consider what happened between Abraham and Sarah. Sarah thought that a "Plan B" was necessary to fulfill God's promise to her husband. The Bible doesn't give us a word-for-word description of her conversation with Abraham, but I'm sure it went something like this: "Look, Abraham, we both know that God has promised to make you the father of many nations. But we also know that I'm well past the age when I can have a baby. But Hagar, my hand-maiden, now there's a woman who is still in the prime of life. She could be the one to have your baby. I really think you should think seriously about that." (See Genesis 16:1.)

Abraham, like millions of other husbands before and since his day, was willing to do just about anything his wife wanted him to do; so he slept with Hagar. She became pregnant and gave birth to a son whom she named Ishmael. (See Genesis 16:4-16.)

Now, God's promise was; to Abraham and Sarah. It was not necessary to help God out. There was no need to put a "Plan B" into place; but when they did, the whole thing backfired terribly. The situation led to strife between Sarah and Hagar, and then between the descendants of Ishmael and Isaac. (See Genesis 25:18.) That strife has continued for centuries, for through Isaac the Jewish race descended, and through Ishmael the Arab nation was born. Certainly, it was Sarah's (and Abraham's) rashness in believing that they had to help God out by devising a "Plan B" that led to centuries of trouble.

You may remember another time when someone thought there was a need for a "Plan B" and it resulted in a whole bunch of trouble. That someone was Aaron, the brother of Moses. Moses had gone up on the mountain to receive instruction from the Lord, including the Ten Commandments. In his absence, the people of Israel grew impatient. They didn't know if Moses was coming back. They were tired of following after an "invisible" God. They wanted something they could see and touch, so Aaron gathered up all the gold from the people, melted it down, fashioned it into the shape of a calf, and presented it to them as the god who had brought them out of Egypt. (See Exodus 32:1.)

Such blasphemy! They had seen the plagues God had brought upon the nation of Egypt. They had seen Him part the Red Sea so they could pass through it and then bring the waves crashing down on the heads of the Egyptians who tried to pursue them. They had seen the pillar of fire by night and the cloud of smoke by day, leading them to the Promised Land, but still, they were ready to trade the glory of the living God for a statue of a cow! Talk about trading a glorious "Plan A" for a pathetic "Plan B." And, of course, the results were disastrous.

In the world of faith, there is simply no need to have "Plan B" in your back pocket, because God s "Plan A" *always* works. The most important thing is to spend time praying and meditating on the Word so you have a clear understanding of "Plan A."

I admit that it isn't always easy to follow God's plan for your life. There will be times when, from a natural perspective, it may be downright scary. But you've got to keep your eyes focused on

Jesus instead of on the wind and the waves. No matter what your circumstances appear to be, God is with you.

> *Be strong and courageous, do not be afraid or tremble at them, for the LORD your God is the one who goes with you. He will not fail you or forsake you.*   (Deuteronomy 31:6 NASB)

One of the most common reasons why people give up on "Plan A" and start casting about for Plans B and C is that they are too impatient. They want to follow God's plan, but they want it to unfold quickly and immediately. They want it to be what I call a "microwave miracle." They'll say, "Well, I've tried to follow the Lord's plan for my life for a week now and it doesn't seem to be working out, so I think I'll try something else."

I believe this type of thinking is a result of the world in which we live. We have instant coffee, instant potatoes, and instant rice. Microwave ovens can cook in fifteen minutes what used to take an hour or more. Quicker. Faster. Immediate gratification. Those are the buzzwords of modern America, but it doesn't work that way in the realm of the spirit. Some things take time. They involve growth and perseverance. They may involve holding to a promise from God over a period of months or even years!

Abraham believed God's promise for a long time before he saw it come true. We all need to get to the point where we can believe and walk in the word of the Lord no matter what we see around us. Talk to yourself if you have to: "Soul, God said this, and this is the way we are going to go."

Your soul may answer you back, "Well, what about money? What about security for your family?" What about a hundred other things? In the natural, these are all legitimate questions, but the word of the Lord is above all that. God's ways are higher than man's ways. His thoughts are higher than man's thoughts. His plans for us are better than the plans we could devise for ourselves.

(See Isaiah 55:9; Jeremiah 29:11.) Don't go looking for microwave miracles. Hold fast to God's "Plan A" for your life. Walk in it and become stable in it!

Walking in Patience

> *But let patience have her perfect work, that ye may be perfect and entire, wanting nothing.* (James 1:4)

Patience is so important—not only in the realm of the spirit, but in the natural world as well. We can see the different results of patience versus impatience all around us. In the world of finance, a person who saves and invests wisely and carefully will see a steady growth in their net worth. An impatient person who is always looking for a big-money, get-rich-quick scheme is always on the verge of "making it big" but never really does. This is an example of how "slow and steady wins the race."

Consider the many quick weight-loss diets. There are some diets that can help people lose weight almost overnight. But there are a lot of discouraged people walking around who lost a lot of weight in a hurry only to see it all come back in a very short time. It takes patience, proper eating habits, and exercise to keep your body in shape. There are no shortcuts. Patience and perseverance are the keys.

It takes patience to be a good parent. It takes patience to build a strong marriage. It takes patience to strengthen and develop your mind. And it takes patience to wait on the Lord, but it is well worth it.

> *But they that wait upon the LORD shall renew their strength; they shall mount up with wings as eagles; they shall run, and not be weary; and they shall walk, and not faint.* (Isaiah 40:31)

Don't think you are wasting your time by waiting on the Lord. You aren't! You are gaining strength and knowledge for the task ahead of you. Your patience for His perfect timing in your life will pay off.

Now keep in mind that patience isn't the same as inertia. I'm not talking about sitting back for months and being inactive. There is a time for patiently sitting and listening to God, and there is a time for action. When He tells you to move, move! When that time for action comes, don't be afraid. God may be calling you to do something new and different. Sticking with the old ways of doing something does not constitute patience. You can keep up with what God is doing and operate in patience at the same time.

One day, if the Lord tarries, the things that are occurring in the world right now will come to a divine conclusion. Something new will begin to happen, and we will need to be in tune with that, whatever it is. We need to listen to God and be led by His Holy Spirit so we always stay on the cutting edge—always moving forward. God wants us to be patient and to wait on Him, but He doesn't want us to grow fat, complacent, and lazy. His job is to lead. Our job is to follow and hang on tenaciously to His word to us.

Holding on Tight to God's Word

God said to me, "Go to the nations and preach. Write books and I will sell them. Preach strong and I will draw the people. Prophesy and you will have the ability to minister to preachers." God gave that word to me, and as long as I hold to it and follow it, it works. If I ever hold to the operation of that word and let go of the foundation of it, I lose it. In other words, if I ever start thinking that the books I have written are the ultimate thing, then I will lose the word of the Lord that caused them to be born and be successful. I have to hold to the word and not what the word produced.

I was in high school when the Lord first told me to write books. It's not possible to have a better literary agent than Almighty God! As long as I keep writing, trying to get the word of the Lord out to people through the printed page, I know my books will continue to sell. While I don't have a whole lot of time to devote to writing, I work at it a little bit here and a little bit there; and it comes together just the way God told me it would.

Some people say, "I don't understand. Why does this work so well for you?" All I can say is, "I'm just following God!" It's really that simple. God said to write the books and He would get them into the hands of those who could be blessed, encouraged, and instructed by them. I simply obey Him.

I have been overseas when people have walked up to me and handed me a copy of one of my books printed in a foreign language where I didn't even know it had been translated. I'll have to admit there have been times when I thought, *Now wait a minute. Did I sign a contract authorizing this to be done?* But then I hear God's voice whisper to my spirit: "I didn't say anything about a contract. I just told you to write books, and I would get them into the hands of those I want to read them." You see, for a brief moment I was losing sight of what God had spoken. My goal and objective is that as many people as possible read the prophetic word of God and that He be glorified in all that I do.

By the grace of God, I have over a million books in print in more than a dozen languages. Does that sound like bragging? Well, it's not. The success of my books doesn't reflect on me personally. It reflects on what can happen when you do what God tells you to do.

Some of you are facing challenges and transitions in your life. You may know beyond a shadow of a doubt that God spoke to you and revealed His plan for your life. You have already gone through the time of wondering, *Is this really God?* You *know* it was God who spoke to you. Now is the time to hold to the word He gave you. Don't waver or doubt, but let that word manifest itself in your life.

Remember the faith of Abraham. Even as he was placing Isaac on the altar, he was holding tightly to the word God had given him. He knew that even if Isaac's life was offered up as a sacrifice, God could bring the boy back from the dead in order to fulfill His word that Abraham would be the father of many nations.

If you are going through a drastic change in your life, things may not have gone the way you thought they were going to go, and you don't see how they're going to change. It's easy to become sad, angry, and frustrated and then let go of God's word and run back to the comfort of yesterday and the way things used to be. Don't do it! Hold on to God's word to you, and believe that He is able to raise your Isaac from the dead.

There have been times when the Isaac in my life was dead, and the only thing I had to hang on to was my faith in what God had said to me. When it would have been easier to say, "I quit," I had to stand and say, "I believe." I knew I couldn't quit. I had to hang on and remind myself that God is always faithful. There was nothing else to say or do. I just had to believe that God's word to me was true and I would see, in due season, the fruit it would produce.

> *I know whom I have believed, and am persuaded that he is able to keep that which I have committed unto him against that day.*   (2 Timothy 1:12)

You can have great assurance in the knowledge that God will finish whatever work He has begun in you. He will finish it if you will hold to your faith and be persuaded that He is able to perform what He said He would do. He is able to fulfill every one of His promises. God wants that for you today. Hold to it! God is not dead, but alive. He is all-mighty and not all-weak.

> *For I am confident of this very thing, that He who began a good work in you will perfect it until the day of Christ Jesus.*
>   (Philippians 1:6 NASB)

What is the word the Lord has put into your heart? Don't look at your present circumstances, but find the word in your spirit. Right now, begin to pray that word. Stir it up. Keep it alive. Pray strong on that word. Let it live again! His plans for your future are absolutely glorious! You can count on it!

THE QUEST FOR
SPIRITUAL HUNGER

By Roberts Liardon

CONTENTS

1

DEVELOPING A SPIRITUAL HUNGER

Blessed are they which do hunger and thirst after
righteousness: for they shall be filled.
—Matthew 5:6

In keeping with Jewish custom, Jesus' parents went to Jerusalem for the feast of the Passover every year. When he was twelve years old, His family made their annual trip to Jerusalem for the feast; and when the feast was over, Jesus' parents started the return trip home, unaware Jesus was not with them. The boy Jesus stayed behind in Jerusalem because of His great interest in the affairs of His heavenly Father. At the tender age of twelve, Jesus hungered for the things of the Spirit of God.

Thinking Jesus was in their company, His family traveled on for a day. Finally realizing He wasn't with them, they began looking among their relatives and friends, and when they did not find Him, they went back to Jerusalem. After three days, they found Him in the temple courts, sitting among the teachers, listening to them, and asking them questions. Everyone who heard Jesus was amazed at His understanding of the Scriptures. The wisdom in Jesus at this age baffled the godly leaders of Jerusalem.

When his parents saw him, they were astonished. His mother said to him, "Son, why have you treated us like this? Your father and I have been anxiously searching for you." "Why were you searching for me?" he asked. "Didn't you know I had to be in my Father's house?" But they did not understand what he was saying to them. Then he went down to Nazareth with them and was obedient to them. But his mother treasured all these things in her heart. And Jesus grew in wisdom and stature, and in favor with God and men. (Luke 2:48–52 NIV)

His spiritual wisdom also baffled his parents. At twelve years of age, Jesus was already about kingdom business. The most important business you can attend to is your heavenly Father's business, no matter what your age. This is the hour when children, even those younger than twelve, will step forth into kingdom business as leaders!

When I first started walking with God, everybody told me the things I could not do. No one told me the things I could do. But there was such a hunger on the inside of me! I still have that hunger for the things of God, and I want God big—not small. I was taught as a child that God is big, and you have to pay a price to get Him. Salvation is a free gift, but there is more than being born again and going to heaven. You must pay a price to get that "something more."

I remember sometimes I would say to my mother or my grandmother, "I don't want to read the Bible. I think it's boring. I don't want to pray anymore. I think that's boring too."

They would respond, "That's what you think!" Then they would get after me.

Grandma trained me. A lot of people do not have grandparents or parents to train them as I did, but Grandma was persistent in training me. She helped develop a spiritual hunger in me. If there were more teachers like my grandmother, we would live in a better world. We would be taught how to live in the realm of the spirit continually, the realm where Christians are supposed to live.

The glory of God rarely comes for many, and often people don't flow with the Holy Spirit because they do not hunger for the things of God.

Developing a Spiritual Appetite

A mental desire to see the spectacular is not spiritual hunger but rather a soulish desire. A mental desire will not get you to the place where you will be led by the Holy Spirit, nor will it help you flow with the Holy Spirit. Operating from a mental desire is not being led by the Holy Spirit. You must make yourself "eat" righteousness until your appetite desires more righteousness. Grandma made me "eat" righteousness. She made me "eat" John 3:16. She made me read my Bible from cover to cover every year that she had charge of me. If I was not reading the Word, I was hearing the Word. She continually played cassette tapes of spiritual teaching and preaching. Television was monitored. Music was monitored. The Word of God prevailed in our home to the point where there was nothing else to see or hear but the things of righteousness.

We fellowshipped with people who possessed spiritual hunger, and we were not allowed to associate with people who did not desire the things of God. I did not realize the forces of evil that Grandma kept off me until she finally turned me loose. Once she released me from her protective authority, those forces hit me hard. I thought, *Grandma, let me get back under your control. It's easier there.*

She said, "No. Now you must grow up and be a man."

Grandma had wisdom regarding spiritual training. Now that I am older, I have not departed from the way of righteousness. Because

Grandma loved me, she trained me to hunger and thirst after righteousness, not after the things of the world. The desire for righteousness got into my blood and now I desire the things of the Spirit.

Television was monitored. Music was monitored. Our home was like a military academy in some ways; however, divine love flowed freely, causing everything to function properly. Problems arise when you do not have love in the home. Love has the same effect as oil in an engine.

Many people try to do what Grandma did, but they use the power of the rod without the oil of love. You will experience problems with teenagers, whether there is discipline or a lack of discipline, if there is no real love and caring involved. Some teenagers rebel at the things of God when they must read the Bible or attend church, because there is plenty of discipline but not enough love in their home. Those parents need to ask God for a greater dimension of His love and express it to their children.

Done in love, the rod means correction. Otherwise, spanking is punishment. All of the Bible verses dealing with bringing up children mean correction or instruction—not punishment.

The natural man has a built-in desire for truth and reality. We are created that way. Most of the time, however, we are "programmed" by the world's thinking and the world's system into accepting a counterfeit so that the world's "truth and reality" are really falsehood and unreality.

Because of Grandma's correction and instruction, I enjoyed the Bible by the time she placed me on my own. I enjoyed hearing about the deep things of God. I hungered for the things of the Spirit. She had fed my natural desire for truth and kept me from the world s counterfeit.

Many parents say, "What is wrong with our children? We've trained them, but somewhere something went wrong." You cannot say you have trained your children if you have been setting a wrong example in front of them. You cannot simply *tell* your children what to do. You must *show* them by example. Much of Grandma's instruction found a home in me because she showed me, by the way she led her life, the truths she taught.

It is time for the body of Christ to wake up and walk in God's truth. Too many Christians are playing games with God, not hungering or thirsting for His righteousness. Then they wonder why their children throw off their training.

I saw people in Africa die because they were physically hungry. But even those Africans who were not starving had a hunger for sweets because they have little of that sort of food. We took candy into Mozambique to give to the children. Some of them had never seen a piece of candy, but once they heard about it or tasted it, they developed a hunger for it. They wanted it!

The man who took us into the little village in Mozambique warned us, "Be careful with that candy because the children will jump you for it."

Not heeding his words of wisdom, I pulled the bag of candy out of my pocket and asked the children, "Do you want a piece?"

There were only three pieces of candy in my hand, but they knew I had more. The children could not understand a word I said, but one of the people with me yelled, "Roberts, be careful!"

I thought, *What can these little kids do to me?*

Holding my hand down to the children, I looked at the candy to see how fast it would go—but I did not know my fingers would go with it! They began hitting my hand and pulling on my fingers for more. Those children hungered after that candy! They wanted it! I began to pray, "Lord, help me get loose from these children." Finally, I managed to get back in the truck, get the door closed, and get someone to join me on the other side of the seat. I said,

"Here is the bag of candy. Count to three, grab as much as you can, and throw it out the door. That way, we'll be safe."

Your hunger for God should be no different. If you do not hunger after the things of God as those children hungered for candy, when the things of God come to you, you will not recognize them.

Why are people missing the moves of God that are happening in their midst right now? Not hungering or thirsting for the things of God makes it easy to miss what God is doing. The African children hungered after that candy. That is how we need to be with the things of God—enjoying what we now have but constantly hungering for more. We need to want more of God, His presence, His glory, and His power. We need to want to talk with Him as a friend. We need to want more of Him in every part of our lives!

There came a day when Grandma said, "Now, it's up to you." She was firm and determined with me, so the only thing I knew to do was what she did—press in for more of the things of God.

I would walk the floor, saying, "I want more of You, God. Holy Spirit, flow through me. Holy Spirit, lead me, teach me, and guide me. I want more of You. I want all I can get, and then I want some more."

How long do you have to walk the floor and say that until you start desiring the things of God? Sometimes it takes months. Set your mind on the things of God. Make your mouth declare your hunger for God. I made myself do this. I did not want to at first, but I did it anyway. Now, I have more of God. I have Him all over me, in me, out of me, and around me.

I spoke these things until I developed a hunger for God. He will answer you when He sees that you have a true hunger for Him. As I walked the floor in prayer, I was developing my inner man—my spirit man.

By the Holy Spirit in my spirit, I began calling those things which were not as though they were. I received more of God. The gifts of the Holy Spirit began to flow through me. I began to see visions. My spiritual hunger increased continually, and I still want more of God.

A Hunger for Righteousness

When I was in Africa, I wanted an American hamburger so badly I could almost see a McDonald's restaurant. I enjoyed and ate African food, but I was hungry for a hamburger. When I arrived back in the United States at the Tulsa International Airport, I did not say, "Hello," or "It's good to see you." I asked, "Where's a McDonald's? I want a hamburger and I want it now!" A specific hunger had developed in me that nothing else satisfied. I got a McDonald's hamburger, devoured it, and went back for another one.

Blessed are they which do hunger and thirst after righteousness: for they shall be filled. (Matthew 5:6)

There are all kinds of hunger, but there is only one hunger that God wants us to have—the hunger for righteousness. How long do you have to hunger like this before God answers you? Until there is a proven hunger.

Some folks satisfy their hunger with the false; other people give up too easily. I could have given up my hunger for a hamburger while I traveled through Africa, but I kept it. I knew that hamburger was out there somewhere. I got to the point where I was willing to take a morning flight, eat a hamburger, and fly back! I really wanted a hamburger. Do you understand that kind of hunger? I would probably have given one hundred dollars for a hamburger that cost only a dollar or two. I wanted one.

To be spiritually filled and to have spiritual growth, you must hunger after the things of God. Grandma developed that kind of hunger in me. After I was on my own, I continued to develop that hunger—I became starved for more of God.

Spiritual Hunger Can Be Satisfied but Never Vanquished

After you attain your goal, spiritual hunger always reaches for more. I have tried to imagine what the things of God will be like in the next move of His Spirit. What will happen to people when the glory hits? How will I react? The glory is just now beginning to hit a little here and there. Yet even now, people are being turned away from meetings because there is no room. Ministries are beginning to explode with growth.

I believe my ministry is beginning to explode because at nine and ten years of age I was saying, "I want more of God. I hunger after God. I am thirsty for God's living water. I am thirsty for God's knowledge. I am hungry for the things of God." The Bible promises that you shall be filled, yet the hunger for God never comes to an end—it goes on forever. To go to the next realm of glory, you must be filled with the one where you are.

Many people get saved and baptized in the Holy Spirit, believe in healing, know the Word works, and they are happy, but they stay on the same level of glory, which results in a spiritual bloating, not spiritual growth. They do not look for a new realm of glory because they are content where they are. While they are feasting in one realm of glory, their eyes should be looking for the next realm of glory. That is the way they need to be to flow with the Spirit of God.

True spiritual hunger will cause you to devour the Word of God and go back for more. Spiritual hunger recognizes real spiritual food. You will recognize the genuine, and you will recognize the counterfeit. Spiritual hunger will cause the things in the natural realm to become less significant in your life.

The Russians know that if the people are hungry, they will be easy to rule. Once they bring food, the starving people will do anything the authorities say and think whatever the rulers want them to think. A starving people can be the most militant, mean, and successful force on the earth. If we are desirous of the things of God, we must be very militant in getting them. That means we will break down the doors of darkness to get the true light.

Truly Hungry People Are Violent People

Starving people are violent people. If you are not "violent" where spiritual food is concerned, you are not truly hungry. If I said to some people, "I hunger for the things of God," they would think I am weird. But you have to be like that. I believe this kind of spiritual hunger was what Jesus had in mind when He said:

> And from the days of John the Baptist until now the kingdom
> of heaven suffereth violence, and the violent take it by force.
> (Matthew 11:12)

Teenagers, listen to me: You need to walk the floor, confess the Word, and meditate on the Word. Even if it seems strange, meditate on God and on the things of God. Let the Holy Spirit put visions in your mind of the plans God has for you.

I have meditated on the outreaches of Roberts Liardon Ministries for years. I have meditated on missionary work for years. I have meditated on my traveling ministry for years. I would see myself enlarging my circles all the time. I would see myself overseas preaching to the masses. I would see myself building up the people. I have dreamed and dreamed and dreamed until today these things are beginning to happen. Yet, I am still hungering for more.

> *Deep calleth unto deep.*   (Psalm 42:7)

If there is a deep calling, there must be a deep to answer the call. If there is a hunger, there must be something to satisfy the hunger. If you are hungering for more power, there must be power to receive. If you are hungering for more love, there must be more love to receive.

The late evangelist William Branham told the story of a little boy who ate things containing sulfur. Once, he ate his bicycle pedal. That sounds extreme! They took him to the doctor who found that the little boy's body craved sulfur so much that he ate things containing it, not knowing why or even knowing those things contained sulfur.

I have seen African pastors hunger for the things of God in a similar manner, and some of them have only one or two pages of the Bible. Yet they are doing all the right things, not knowing they are following principles of the Word of God. As a result, they are getting blessed.

That is the way all Christians are supposed to be. We are to hunger after the things of God and not search or hunger after anything or anyone but God. The Bible says that if we hunger after God, we will be filled. If you hunger after spiritual things, God will make sure we have everything we need in the natural.

God satisfies my every desire. I am happy with the clothes I wear, the money He provides, and the traveling I do. I am happy with the ministry God has given me. I believe the reason God satisfies my every need is because I hunger after Him more every day.

Spiritual Hunger Brings Blessings

If you want to be blessed in the natural realm, get your eyes on God. Get your hunger off of cars, homes, and bank accounts, and get it on God. Now, I am not looking for a large, personal bank account, but if it comes, I am not going to be dumb enough to turn it down. Some people think that being spiritual means rejecting every material blessing. But God says He causes the wealth of the wicked to come into our hands.

A good man leaveth an inheritance to his children's children: and the wealth of the sinner is laid up for the just.

(Proverbs 13:22)

When wealth comes, I am certainly not going to return it! I will receive it in Jesus' name.

As I walk and hunger after the things of God, He gives me everything I need. I am trying to carry you to a new level of spiritual hunger. Look for God in everything!

2

MATURATION IN THE SCHOOL OF THE HOLY SPIRIT

Regardless of your natural age, once you have developed a spiritual hunger, paid a visit to the Father's house, and received His direction for your life, a time of preparation must take place before you step into your call. I have seen people ignore the need for preparation time or abort this special time only to end up on the spiritual trash heap—no good to anyone because they were not spiritually ready for their particular assignment.

God's timing is as important as His call.

It is not God's intent for anyone to end up defeated from not knowing how to battle daily the evil elements of the world. I have seen this type of defeat overtake far too many of God's chosen, called, anointed, and commissioned vessels.

Whatever God has called you to do will require both natural and spiritual preparation. However, natural preparation without adequate spiritual preparation will not work. Spiritual preparation cannot be shirked. Little or no preparation sets the stage for a difficult time in undertaking any assignment from on high. You will get discouraged more easily and give up if your spiritual preparation is not adequate. You will end up doing nothing for God.

I have seen people go off to Bible school, and after a short time of preparation and training, they think they are ready to conquer the entire world! After this natural preparation in the knowledge of the Word, they need the spiritual preparation in the school of the Holy Spirit, attained only on their knees in prayer.

There is more to preparation than going to Bible school. I do not want to see more young, anointed ministers of the gospel devastated beyond repair and losing the harvest of souls they were to gather because of being spiritually ill prepared.

Learn Spiritual Things Early

My grandmother is an old-time Pentecostal who, as a teenager, attended an Akron, Ohio, church where "hellfire and brimstone" were preached. Her church taught that you would not go to heaven unless you were baptized in the Holy Spirit. (Thank the Lord, we have come a long way since that time.) Grandma met people in her church who had been a part of the Azusa Street revival—the beginning of modern-day Pentecostalism.

The pastor of this church began a twenty-four-hour prayer chain, and Grandma volunteered to pray an hour a day as part of this chain. People in her day seemed to be more committed than many believers are today. It is difficult to get people to pray three seconds for the church or for anything else. Eternal things merit far more importance than natural things, and we need to spend more time developing the things of the Spirit in our lives.

Grandmas father taught her, "Never tell a lie. Once you have given your word, stick to it at any cost"—a good philosophy for everyone. We need that preached more often from our local church pulpits. Once you say you will do something, be willing to die to keep your word. Your word is your bond. Don't let it float around with no meaning or commitment attached.

Grandma gave her word that she would pray an hour a day as part of Reverend McKinney s prayer chain. She would set her clock for an hour, but after praying for everything she could think of, she found that only ten minutes had passed. Prayer requires discipline and just like exercise, you become better with practice.

Grandma said, "I would not give up because I had committed myself to that hour. I told that man of God that I would pray an hour for his church, so I was going to do it or die." And she thought she was going to die! She would pray about everything she knew to pray about, which back then included only her neighbors, the mayor, policemen, prostitutes, and unsaved loved ones. She was involved in her own little world. However, Grandma hungered and thirsted for the things of God, and it was during this time she developed into a mighty prayer warrior. The minute she hit her knees in prayer, the Holy Spirit came on the scene. That is what we should all be striving for.

Teaching by Example

Grandma always enforced what Jesus said. I will never forget the day she looked at me and said, "Whether you are going to be a successful businessman or a minister of the gospel, you must know how to pray. So let's begin right now." She did not even ask me if I wanted to pray. She made me pray. She dragged me into a prayer life. The first day, I did not want to pray. Like any other kid, I wanted to watch television. Thank God that Grandma was persistent.

She said, "Get on your knees." I obeyed. I was very young at the time.

"Throw your hands up and praise God," she told me. I did.

She said, "Repeat after me," then led me in my first Holy Spirit prayer and never said "Amen;" she just started praying on her own.

Kneeling down beside me, she would say, "I don't want you to move from this spot. If you do, when I get through praying, you are going to get it!"

Grandma would pray for hours. She meant business when she prayed. She would pray, "God, help our churches to honor the Bible. Fill the preachers with Holy Spirit fire. If they do not honor You, remove them from the pulpits. Get Holy Spirit men in the pulpits, not dead ones."

We need that kind of praying today. Grandma knew that dead preachers produce dead people. Fiery preachers produce fire in the church, fire for God, and fire for the things of God. Hallelujah! I have seen Grandma literally "pray in" revivals.

When Grandma came against the forces of darkness in prayer, that is when things would get interesting. When she started fighting demons, that is when I became interested. My sister and I watched her. I learned a lot by watching her, and your children will learn best by your example. They will learn best by seeing you pray, by seeing you fight the forces of darkness, and by seeing you intercede for others.

I thought everyone prayed like Grandma. It was a shock when I found out that few Christians pray at all. I wondered what was wrong with everyone else's grandmothers. I wondered what was wrong with their homes. I was trained in spiritual things in my home by my grandmother and my mother. I was not told, "Go to your room, pray, and read the Scripture by yourself." Grandma showed me how to pray. She took me with her into the realm of the spirit. She showed me how to fight demonic forces, how to get the bills paid, and how to pray the right people into positions of leadership and the wrong ones out.

You can best show others how to be led by the Spirit of God through the life you live, not by what you say. Talk is cheap, especially in children's eyes. If you are not living what you say you believe, children will not buy what you say.

Grandma always told me, "Don't ever be ashamed of the gospel. Don't ever be ashamed to yield to the Holy Spirit, wherever you are."

It was normal for Grandma to walk down the aisles in the grocery store praying in tongues. One night, God spoke to me in a grocery store and told me to cast the devil out of someone. I flinched a little, but I obeyed. I learned early on that it is best to obey! When children are trained right, they will not depart from the ways of the Lord when they get old. (See Proverbs 22:6.) If you want Holy-Spirit-trained children, open your eyes and ears to what the Spirit of God is saying.

I am really tired of seeing my generation all goofed up. In most cases, it is the fault of parents who did not train their children in the ways of God while they were young.

Unity and Corporate Prayer

If any member of Grandma's family faced a situation where he or she couldn't seem to pray through to victory, another family member was called and they prayed in agreement until the battle was won. It is the same in the body of Christ. When one family member hurts, we all hurt until we pray the situation through to victory.

We have agreed together in prayer until everyone's bills were paid. We have stood together until we saw answers to prayer. We have hounded heaven's doors until God answered. I believe sometimes God must have said, "Let's answer their prayers so they will be quiet!" We knew how to be persistent in prayer, which is one of the keys to a successful prayer life. Confession is important, but it must be reinforced with prayer to be effective.

I am convinced that corporate prayer, unity, and love are God's design for the entire body of Christ. Only in this manner will we overcome some of the hurdles we face in this day and hour. God is calling men and women to use power and discernment—sharpened through prayer. Then, everywhere we walk, we will tear the devil up.

> But ye, beloved, building up yourselves on your most holy faith, praying in the Holy Ghost, keep yourselves in the love of God, looking for the mercy of our Lord Jesus Christ unto eternal life.   (Jude 20–21)

I believe Grandma knew these verses very well because when we came home from school, she would take us in a room, shut the door, and say, "Now, hit your knees. I want to hear you pray in tongues loud enough for both your ears and mine to hear." Why did she do that? Although it seemed weird at first, that attitude strengthened us in the boldness of the Lord.

If we did not pray loud enough, she would say, "I can't hear you!"

That is how to train your children in the ways of the Lord. That is how to teach them about the realm of the spirit. Teach them to discern a demon from an angel. In prayer your children learn to know the voice of God from a human or demonic voice.

Grandma knew how to raise children, and she knew how to build churches. She would head up prayer groups and teach them exactly as she taught me. She would set the example of how to pray, and she would correct in love when someone got in the flesh. As a result, the power of the Holy Spirit cleaned up both the individuals and the church.

Spiritual Training Begins in the Home

I am convinced that God ordained the training program, through which Grandma put me, for parents, not for Sunday school teachers, nursery school teachers, or Christian school teachers. The training of a child's spirit must begin in the home.

My early life consisted mostly of Grandma, God, me, and my bedroom. That is when I learned to pray. The day came when Grandma no longer had to push me into spiritual things, particularly in prayer. I had learned to enjoy praying with great boldness. I desired to pray in the Spirit and everything else became secondary. I hungered for the things of the Spirit.

The day came when I would say, "Grandma, let's go pray." She would answer, "We haven't had breakfast yet!"

I would respond, "I don't care. Let's pray, Grandma. Let's go set people free from devils! Let's pray for the man next door."

I would pray as long as I could and get as close to Grandma as I could because the closer I was to her, the more I would be in the midst of the power of God when it fell. I wanted Grandma to get into that realm. I wanted the glory of God to hit. I enjoyed shaking under the power of God. I knew I would be strengthened when the glory hit.

When we prayed, I would make sure Grandma was comfortable. I would make sure she had her glass of water, her handkerchief, and her pillows. I would make sure the phone was off the hook. I would make sure no one came to the door. I knew prayer time was a time when we did not want to be disturbed in any way. No interruptions were allowed. That was the standard Grandma set.

When she prayed, I knew what every little grunt meant, and I would go get what she wanted. That is the way ministries need to treat the prophets of God today. A sigh from Grandma, a move of her little finger, and I knew what that meant. I knew Grandma better than anyone else knew her. That is the way you should be when a man or woman of God comes across your pathway. By the Spirit of God, you will know what is needed and what to say.

Grandma would discern through the Holy Spirit when family members had difficulties, even those who lived a great distance away. She would pray and we would soon see the manifestation of her prayers. Family members in difficulty were soon restored to God. Grandma had a "hotline" to God, and I knew it by the fruit of her labor. The Word of God says,

> The eyes of the LORD are upon the righteous, and his ears are open unto their cry. The face of the LORD is against them that do evil, to cut off the remembrance of them from the earth. The righteous cry, and the LORD heareth, and delivereth them out of all their troubles.   (Psalm 34:15–17)

To survive in this hour, we must be keenly tuned to the Spirit of God. Grandma sharpened my human spirit to hear the Spirit of God as I became her "Elisha." You need to train your children to be your "Elishas."

Elisha knew everything about Elijah. When it was time for Elijah to go home to heaven, he asked Elisha, "What do you want of me? You have been a great blessing to me. You have helped me fight the battles. You have helped me run the race well. Now, what can I do for you?" (See 2 Kings 2:9.)

> And it came to pass, when the LORD would take up Elijah into heaven by a whirlwind, that Elijah went with Elisha from Gilgal. And Elijah said unto Elisha, Tarry here, I pray thee; for the LORD hath sent me to Bethel. And Elisha said unto him, As the LORD liveth, and as thy soul liveth, I will not leave

thee. So they went down to Bethel And the sons of the prophets that were at Bethel came forth to Elisha, and said unto him, Knowest thou that the LORD will take away thy master from thy head to day? And he said, Yea, I know it: hold ye your peace. And Elijah said unto him, Elisha, tarry here, I pray thee; for the Lord hath sent me to Jericho. And he said, As the LORD liveth, and as thy soul liveth, I will not leave thee. So they came to Jericho. And the sons of the prophets that were at Jericho came to Elisha, and said unto him, Knowest thou that the LORD will take away thy master from thy head to day? And he answered, Yea, I know it: hold ye your peace. And Elijah said unto him, Tarry, I pray thee, here; for the LORD hath sent me to Jordan. And he said, As the LORD liveth, and as thy soul liveth, I will not leave thee. And they two went on. And fifty men of the sons of the prophets went, and stood to view afar off: and they two stood by Jordan. And Elijah took his mantle, and wrapped it together, and smote the waters, and they were divided hither and thither, so that they two went over on dry ground. And it came to pass, when they were gone over, that Elijah said unto Elisha, Ask what I shall do for thee, before I be taken away from thee. And Elisha said, I pray thee, let a double portion of thy spirit be upon me. And he said, Thou hast asked a hard thing: nevertheless, if thou see me when I am taken from thee, it shall be so unto thee; but if not, it shall not be so. And it came to pass, as they still went on, and talked, that, behold, there appeared a chariot of fire, and horses of fire, and parted them both asunder; and Elijah went up by a whirlwind into heaven. And Elisha saw it, and he cried, My father, my father, the chariot of Israel, and the horsemen thereof. And he saw him no more: and he took hold of his own clothes, and rent them in two pieces. He took up also the mantle of Elijah that fell from him, and went back and stood by the bank of Jordan; and he took the mantle of Elijah that fell from him, and smote the waters, and said, Where is the Lord *God of Elijah? and when he also had smitten the waters, they parted hither and thither: and Elisha went over. And when the sons of the prophets which were to view at Jericho saw him, they said,* **The spirit of Elijah doth rest on Elisha.** *And they came to meet him, and bowed themselves to the ground before him.*   (2 Kings 2:1–15)

Elisha asked for a double portion of Elijah's spirit. He wanted all that Elijah had and more, and Elisha went on to do many great miracles for God throughout the rest of his life. This came about as a result of the training he had received from Elijah. There was a time of preparation Elisha went through before God could give him Elijah's mantle. Parents need to put their children through a time of preparation the way my Grandma did me, but even before that, they need to develop their own hunger for God.

3

SIN SQUELCHES SPIRITUAL HUNGER

God wants a glorious church—one without wrinkle, or blemish. The spots, wrinkles, and blemishes are the sins of the believers, not the sins of unbelievers.

Sin is a killer! It will squelch spiritual hunger and block the flow of the Holy Spirit in your life. In fact, sin will halt the move of the Holy Spirit in your life. In studying the lives of great preachers of the past, I have noticed that many of them lost their power, crowds, families, and even their own lives because of sin. Sin destroyed everything they had.

We need to understand that in God's eyes there is no degree of sin. In today's society, we tend to place degrees on sins, thinking, *This one isn't too bad, but this other one is simply horrible.*

Blessed is the man that walketh not in the counsel of the ungodly, nor standeth in the way of sinners, nor sitteth in the seat of the scornful. But his delight is in the law of the Lord; *and in his law doth he meditate day and night. And he shall be like a tree planted by the rivers of water, that bringeth forth his fruit in his season; his leaf also shall not wither; and whatsoever he doeth shall prosper.*

(Psalm 1:1–3)

The Desire to Live a Holy Life

God's Word has a lot to say about living a holy and righteous life. If you truly hunger after the things of the Spirit of God, you will desire to live a holy life.

> Praise ye the LORD. Blessed is the man that feareth the LORD, that delighteth greatly in his commandments. His seed shall be mighty upon earth: the generation of the upright shall be blessed. Wealth and riches shall be in his house: and his righteousness endureth for ever.   (Psalm 112:1–3)

> Blessed are the undefiled in the way, who walk in the law of the LORD. Blessed are they that keep his testimonies, and that seek him with the whole heart.   (Psalm 119:1–2)

It is God's desire that we be "perfect" in Him.

> Thou shalt be perfect with the LORD thy God.
> (Deuteronomy 18:13)

God speaks to us about letting the light of Christ radiate through us.

> Let your light so shine before men, that they may see your good works, and glorify your Father which is in heaven.
> (Matthew 5:16)

> And they shall call them, The holy people, The redeemed of the LORD: and thou shalt be called, Sought out, a city not forsaken.   (Isaiah 62:12)

The kingdom of heaven is prepared for the holy.

> Know ye not that the unrighteous shall not inherit the kingdom of God? Be not deceived: neither fornicators, nor idolaters,

nor adulterers, nor effeminate, nor abusers of themselves with mankind, nor thieves, nor covetous, nor drunkards, nor revilers, nor extortioners, shall inherit the kingdom of God. And such were some of you: but ye are washed, but ye are sanctified, but ye are justified in the name of the Lord Jesus, and by the Spirit of our God. (1 Corinthians 6:9–11)

God tells us to be active in avoiding sin:

But he that is joined unto the Lord is one spirit. Flee fornication. Every sin that a man doeth is without the body; but he that committeth fornication sinneth against his own body. What? know ye not that your body is the temple of the Holy Ghost which is in you, which ye have of God, and ye are not your own? For ye are bought with a price: therefore glorify God in your body, and in your spirit, which are God's.

(1 Corinthians 6:17–20)

God spoke through Paul saying, "*Awake to righteousness.*" That is a command, not an option!

Awake to righteousness, and sin not; for some have not the knowledge of God: I speak this to your shame.

(1 Corinthians 15:34)

Paul continued to write on the theme of holy living in his letter to the church at Galatia.

Be not deceived; God is not mocked: for whatsoever a man soweth, that shall he also reap. For he that soweth to his flesh shall of the flesh reap corruption; but he that soweth to the Spirit shall of the Spirit reap life everlasting. And let us not be weary in well doing: for in due season we shall reap, if we faint not. (Galatians 6:7–9)

In essence, Paul was saying, "We are not called to filth; we are called to holiness."

For God hath not called us unto uncleanness, but unto holiness. (1 Thessalonians 4:7)

The theme of holiness is also discussed by the apostle Peter:

But as he which hath called you is holy, so be ye holy in all manner of conversation; because it is written, Be ye holy; for I am holy. (1 Peter 1:15–16)

Most believers have their outward men well organized to avoid sin. However, internal, "mental" sins will kill them if they are not dealt with.

Let not *sin therefore reign in your mortal body, that ye should obey it in the lusts thereof. Neither yield ye your members as instruments of unrighteousness unto sin: but yield yourselves unto God, as those that are alive from the dead, and your members as instruments of righteousness unto God. For sin shall not have dominion over you: for ye are not under the law, but under grace. What then? shall we sin, because we are not under the law, but under grace? God forbid. Know ye not, that to whom ye yield yourselves servants to obey, his servants ye are to whom ye obey; whether of sin unto death, or of obedience unto righteousness?* (Romans 6:12–16)

In verse 12, "let not" indicates that it is the believer's decision to sin or not to sin. *"Let not"* has everything to do with your personal will. *You* are the one who chooses whether to live a life of holiness and righteousness or a life of sin.

Sin Begins in the Mind

The devil cannot *make* you sin. The only thing the devil can do is offer you the *temptation* to sin. He puts the sin before you. However, you are the one who makes the decision, "Am I going to yield to sin or to God?"

> *Ye have heard that it was said by them of old time, Thou shalt not commit adultery: but I say unto you, That whosoever looketh on a woman to lust after her hath committed adultery with her already in his heart.*   (Matthew 5:27–28)

In this Scripture, Jesus is speaking of mental sins. The mind must be renewed and transformed by the washing of the Word of God. Only then will you be rid of sinful thoughts and imaginations. A wandering mind may think an evil thought, such as adultery, but as believers, we are to think on those things which are true, honest, pure, lovely, and of a good report. (See Philippians 4:8.)

Sin will cause you to lose God's power and block your communication line to the throne room of God. God's glory and sin simply will *not* mix. They will never mix! Shake yourself free from sin completely so you are prepared to taste of God's glory and live. If sin is not dealt with, when God's glory is released, an explosion will take place resulting in judgment, even death at times. (See Acts 5:1-11.)

Old-time preacher, Jonathan Edwards, preached a famous sermon entitled, "Sinners in the Hands of an Angry God."

When he would preach this sermon, people would quake and shake in the middle of the service. But, contrary to popular opinion, this sermon was not about the wrath of God but about His mercy. Edwards preached about how forbearing God is when our unrighteousness comes into contact with His holiness and about what God has a perfect right to do— but doesn't because He loves us. We need some of that fear of God in our churches today.

You cannot go out and knowingly commit sin with the intention of asking for forgiveness the next morning. No, you cannot! It is just as easy to do what is right as it is to sin, but you must make the decision whether to travel the road of sin or the road of righteousness.

Until you make the decision to live a life of holiness, your travels with God will be nonexistent. You see, there are no "big" or "little" sins with God. In His eyes, sin is sin. When you willfully sin, you sow seed that will grow because the devil will make sure it is watered. That sin will bring forth the same kind of fruit: corruption and death. Just as an apple seed produces apples, if you sow sin, you are going to reap sin. And God does not cause that seed to grow and produce—you do. To develop good fruit, you must sow good seeds of righteousness and see that they are watered with the Word.

What about the sin of ignorance? I used to preach a sermon entitled, "Sin No More," in which I would provide people with an escape route. Everyone loved it! I would say, "If you are ignorant, you can plead ignorance before the throne of God, and He will okay it."

Then God showed me I was wrong. The Spirit of God said to me, "When Jesus went to heaven, He sent the Holy Spirit back to the earth—the great teacher—to guide us into all truth."

Howbeit when he, the Spirit of truth, is come, he will guide you into all truth: for he shall not speak of himself; but whatsoever he shall hear, that shall he speak: and he will shew you things to come. (John 16:13)

The Spirit of God does not experience defeat, failure, or sin. He can only guide us into all truth, victory, and success. If we are led by the Spirit of God in all we do, ignorance is not a viable excuse because the Spirit of God will guide and lead us on the right pathway. We will stay on the right road. Therefore, we have no excuse to continue in sin.

Do not *try* not to sin. Simply make a decision not to sin and stick with your decision. When temptation comes, let the devil keep the temptation. How? Step apart from sin. Separate yourself unto a life of godliness.

> *Be ye not unequally yoked together with unbelievers: for what fellowship hath righteousness with unrighteousness? and what communion hath light with darkness? And what concord hath Christ with Belial? or what part hath he that believeth with an infidel? And what agreement hath the temple of God with idols? for ye are the temple of the living God; as God hath said, I will dwell in them, and walk in them; and I will be their God, and they shall be my people. Wherefore come out from among them, and be ye separate, saith the Lord, and touch not the unclean thing: and I will receive you, and will be a Father unto you, and ye shall be my sons and daughters, saith the Lord Almighty.* (2 Corinthians 6:14–18)

Corportate Sin

One of the most prominent corporate sins is gossip. Where corporate sin abounds, corporate judgment will come. God s army is the only army I know that kills its own wounded. In our natural world, doctors stand by doctors; lawyers stand by lawyers; family members stand by family members. Why can't ministers stand by ministers and believers stand by fellow believers?

King Saul made several attempts to kill David; yet, when Saul died, David wept bitterly.

Tell it not in Gath, publish it not in the streets of Askelon; lest the daughters of the Philistines rejoice, lest the daughters of the uncircumcised triumph.   (2 Samuel 1:20)

David was saying, "Don't tell the other lands our king is dead. Don't tell them how he died. Let's keep it quiet."

That is the way it should be in the church. Don't publish the failures of other ministers and believers. Make sure your own life is right, then pray for that erring brother or sister. It is a sin not to stand by fellow believers and ministers and support them when they are going through a hard time.

As believers, we are to pour on the oil and the wine. We are to bind up the wounds. We are to keep the church glorious. We are to sin no more. We are to live in holiness. We are to do what is right in the eyes of God. We need to have a reverence toward the awesomeness of God—knowing that from His breath can come destruction or blessing.

Having therefore these promises, dearly beloved, let us cleanse ourselves from all filthiness of the flesh and spirit, perfecting holiness in the fear of God.   (2 Corinthians 7:1)

As we aim for holiness as a lifestyle, we will continually hunger for spiritual things. Only as we step aside from sin and from things of the world will we want more of God.

Dear friends, now we are children of God, and what we will be has not yet been made known. But we know that when he appears, we shall be like him, for we shall see him as he is. Everyone who has this hope in him purifies himself just as he is pure.   (1 John 3:2–3 NIV)

What a blessed assurance Jesus gave us in the gospel of John. As we make a decision to lay aside sin and the flesh to hunger and thirst for more of Him, we will be filled.

Jesus replied, I am the Bread of Life. He who comes to Me will never be hungry and he who believes on and cleaves to and trusts in and relies on Me will never thirst any more—at any time.   (John 6:35 AMP)

THE PRICE OF
SPIRITUAL HUNGER

By Roberts Liardon

CONTENTS

FOREWORD

In the most agonizing moment of His life, Jesus cried out to His Father, *"Father, if thou be willing, remove this cup from me: nevertheless not my will, but thine, be done"* (Luke 22:42). The Amplified Bible says, *"Father, if You are willing, remove this cup from Me; yet not My will, but (always) Yours, be done."*

Jesus accepted His cross—dying on Calvary—which provided the way through which all mankind might become part of the family of God. Jesus found no way out of the cross experience. No one else could take His place. He faced his Gethsemane alone. When He was enduring the agony of the cross experience, His disciples fell asleep instead of praying, and Peter later denied that he even knew the Messiah.

> *And there appeared an angel unto him from heaven, strengthening him. And being in an agony he prayed more earnestly: and his sweat was as it were great drops of blood falling down to the ground. And when he rose up from prayer, and was come to his disciples, he found them sleeping for sorrow, and said unto them, Why sleep ye? rise and pray, lest ye enter into temptation.* (Luke 22:43–46)

Today, you and I must face our own cross experiences. That cross is different for each person. Your cross experience will correspond to whatever God asks you to do, but what we all have in common is the fact that we must die to self. To be productive for the kingdom of God, there is no alternative and no way out of dying to self. Jesus said, *"And anyone who does not carry his cross and follow me cannot be my disciple"* (Luke 14:27 NIV).

To reject your cross experience is, literally, to play games with God. To reject your cross experience means that you are not really serious about the things of God, and He is not a top priority with you. When you are willing to die to self—to let your flesh die—you become serious about the things of God. *To die to self is to begin to live!*

There is a price to pay to be fit for the Masters use.

> *If a man therefore purge himself from these, he shall be a vessel unto honour, sanctified, and meet for the masters use, and prepared unto every good work.* (2 Timothy 2:21)

To be acceptable for the Master's use, you must lay aside the weights of anything that would hold you to this earth's realm. You must learn to yield to the Holy Spirit by letting your flesh die and learning to live continually in the realm of the Holy Spirit.

1

LAYING ASIDE
THE WEIGHTS

Wherefore seeing we also are compassed about with so great
a cloud of witnesses, let us lay aside every weight, and the sin
which doth so easily beset us, and let us run with patience the
race that is set before us, Looking unto Jesus the author and
finisher of our faith; who for the joy that was set before him
endured the cross, despising the shame, and is set down at the
right hand of the throne of God.
—Hebrews 12:1–2

God is calling to all saints in this hour, "Lay aside every weight that ties you to the things of the earth. Be loosed from anything that binds you to the things of the earth. Be free of everything that would keep you from fulfilling My call and that would hinder your ability to flow with My Spirit."

I learned something about this message a long time ago when no one seemed to care who I was, when no one knew I had gone to heaven, and when no one knew I had a praying grandmother who continually said, "One day, he'll do something for the kingdom of God."

For six long years, I separated myself unto God. I walked my bedroom floor praying in other tongues—sometimes all night long. When I would go to my room for this special time with the Lord, I would take my Bibles, pads of paper, pencils, and a tape recorder. I wanted to hear from heaven. I stepped aside from many of the activities of my family, neighborhood, and school. I laid aside all sports to spend this time alone with the Lord. Many people thought I was crazy and they did not mind telling me so! Not one person seemed to care that I paced the floor with tears streaming down my face because I wanted to hear from God. I wanted nothing but His divine direction for my life.

As I walked my bedroom floor during those six years, I was confronted with evil spirits. But at the same time, I was confronted with glorious angelic hosts from God's realm who sang and ministered to me, strengthening me in my spirit. During this time of separation I learned something I often heard Kathryn Kuhlman say:

> God is not seeking the golden vessels of this earth. He is not seeking the silver vessels. But He is seeking the plain, ordinary, yielded vessels who will obey whatever He asks them to do.

When God speaks, we are to obey. We are not to ask questions or have committee meetings dominated by the intellects of men and women to discuss spiritual matters. When God speaks, we are to obey instantly, knowing He can be trusted to perform His Word, knowing He is faithful to keep His promises, knowing He delights in quickly fulfilling His promises, and knowing He will never fail us! Any time God speaks, we can be confident that He will follow through to cause the manifestation, or fruit, of what He has spoken to come forth.

If God says, "Jump through the wall," we are not to ask where the hole is—we are to jump and let Him worry about the hole.

That may sound a little ridiculous, but that is how strong our faith and trust in God should be.

In the following passage of Scripture, we can hear God's voice calling to *us* as He challenges the heathen nations to wake up their mighty men and prepare for war:

> *Proclaim ye this among the Gentiles; Prepare war, wake up the mighty men, let all the men of war draw near; let them come up: beat your plowshares into swords and your pruning hooks into spears: let the weak say, Iam strong. Assemble yourselves, and come, all ye heathen, and gather yourselves together round about: thither cause thy mighty ones to come down, O LORD. Let the heathen be wakened, and come up to the valley of Jehoshaphat: for there will I sit to judge all the heathen round about. Put ye in the sickle, for the harvest is ripe: come, get you down; for the press is full, the vats overflow; for their wickedness is great. Multitudes, multitudes in the valley of decision: for the day of the LORD is near in the valley of decision.* (Joel 3:9–14)

God says in this hour, "Wake up the mighty men and women— those who have pure hearts and motives toward Me and who know how to pray in the spirit till victory comes. Wake up those whom the world has despised and rejected because of the traditions of men that are contrary to Me."

In this last outpouring of the Holy Spirit, we will face great battles. We must loose all the chains and weights that have kept us tied to the earth because as we learn to flow with the precious Holy Spirit, we will be out ahead of the battles before they hit!

We must be able to go into the very throne room of God, sit around His conference table, and receive our plans and orders directly from Him. We are standing at a crossroads, both as individual believers and as the church. Every believer and every church body must shake loose from all entanglements of the world to be able to respond with immediacy to God's end-time directives.

Many people have taken a few steps into the realm of the spirit to hear from God but have failed to remain there. Because they have not let go of all worldly entanglements, they cannot receive the fullness of God's specific plans designed just for them.

Those who walk in the flesh will discourage you if you attempt to move completely into the realm of the spirit. They will often say, "Be normal. Don't be weird." Have you ever heard that? What they are really saying is, "Don't be normal. Be like us!"

What weights or entanglements are bogging you down? Is it sports, food, wrong friendships, television, an apathetic attitude, pride, sickness, or debt? Whether it is one of these areas or something else, get rid of it. Step into the liberty wherein Christ has set you free. God's Word provides the way of escape out of every entanglement. Diligently seek God through prayer and His Word so you will be able to flow with His Spirit.

Consider yourself a runner in the race Christ has set before you. No runner with even a thimbleful of sense would weigh himself down before entering a race. He would shake free of everything that might hinder his chances to win. He would want that freedom in order to run his very best.

Paul talked about the race of life. He was talking about dying to the flesh and being free in Christ when he spoke of putting his body under.

> *Know ye not that they which run in a race run all, but one receiveth the prize? So run, that ye may obtain. And every man that striveth for the mastery is temperate in all things. Now they do it to obtain a corruptible crown; but we an incorruptible. I therefore so run, not as uncertainly; so fight I, not as one that beateth the air: but I keep under my body, and*

bring it into subjection: lest that by any means, when I have preached to others, I myself should be a castaway.

(1 Corinthians 9:24–27)

No longer can we run with the world and also run with God. Now longer can we straddle the fence and serve both God and mammon. (See Matthew 6:24.) We must make a choice. We cannot live for God part of the time and for the devil the rest of the time. We must choose whom we will serve.

Ye cannot drink the cup of the Lord, and the cup of devils: ye cannot be partakers of the Lord's table, and of the table of devils. Do we provoke the Lord to jealousy? are we stronger than he? All things are lawful for me, but all things are not expedient: all things are lawful for me, but all things edify not.

(1 Corinthians 10:21–23)

The weights of this world must be laid aside quickly. You and I, God's mighty men and women, must enter the spirit realm weight free to be totally effective for God. We will see and do mighty exploits for Him as we shake free from all the weights of the world.

2

YIELDING TO
THE HOLY SPIRIT

I used to ride on the coattail of my grandmother's spirit. I knew that whenever she moved into the glory world, those goose bumps would pop up on me as well. I knew that if I stayed close enough to her, she could "piggyback" me into the realm of the spirit. But one day, God said, "Now it is *your* fight. Now you will be held accountable for your own spirit."

When that release came, I began to realize what my grandma had kept me from. I began to realize the protection she had been to me. Until that time, my mind had never been confused. I had never known what it was to be tormented by evil spirits because she kept them away from me.

I can remember times when I came home from school as a youngster, and Grandma would abruptly stop me and pray for me before I barely got my nose inside the front door! She saw into the realm of the spirit and saw when I had demonic spirits hovering over me. Thank God for Grandma!

The day came when I had to learn to pray and get into the realm of the spirit for myself. I began to realize that no person or ministry would ever succeed because of a great education, financial success, or connections made by man. These things do not entice the anointing of God to fall upon you because the Holy Spirit causes the anointing to fall as He wills, never as man wills. The Holy Spirit never takes directions from man.

God's anointing comes upon yielded vessels—vessels who totally submit and surrender to the Spirit of God. I had to learn to yield to the Holy Spirit; and as I did, the anointing upon me became stronger. I have learned that yielding to the Holy Spirit and living in the realm of the spirit are progressive. As we mature in Christ, we can yield more fully to the Holy Spirit and live in that realm.

The only way to stay in the realm of the spirit is to spend time alone with God. During the first year that I walked my bedroom floor praying and weeping before God, I would look out the window and see my friends playing baseball. My flesh would say, *You're not accomplishing a thing! Go play baseball with your friends. You are not even getting a single goose bump, Roberts!* (That is the kind of encouragement I received from my mind.)

The truth of the matter is that I did not receive even one goose bump for more than a year! I felt nothing. There was absolutely no response from heaven for more than a year. If most people do not hear from heaven within five minutes, they are ready to give up, quit praying, and start confessing, hoping that will bring immediate results.

Some people get into trouble because they are looking for feelings or because they are seeking the approval of men. You cannot go by feelings or men's approval. The quality of your time spent with God is not based on goose bumps or feelings. Spending time in prayer develops a spiritual maturity which gives you a spiritual confidence—a supernatural knowing that you are doing something worthwhile.

My friends, confession will not work unless it is enforced with prayer. You can confess until you are blue in the face, but unless your prayer life is up to par, your confession will not avail.

I knew, however, that if I persisted with God, He would finally show up. My attitude was this: *I am going to walk this bedroom floor until God shows up or I die!*

Some of you need that kind of persistence to get hold of God. Some of you need old-time Pentecostal persistence that will cause you to pray all night until heaven hits earth. Dead, dried-up religion is not worth a thing. Religion kills the spirit and causes the flesh to prevail.

Criticism and persecution will come as you begin to separate yourself unto God, but you have got to get into the realm of the spirit where you belong. You have to get under the shadow of the Almighty and stay there. You have to get to the place where the winds of God will overshadow you and will carry you.

No weapon that is formed against thee shall prosper; and every tongue that shall rise against thee in judgment thou shalt condemn. This is the heritage of the servants of the Lord, *and their righteousness is of me, saith the* Lord.   (Isaiah 54:17)

When I was a teenager, I talked to God as I walked down the school hallways. I was not concerned about what others thought of me. I was not concerned about a social life or sports. I wanted more of God, and I did not care what it cost me to have a relationship with Him. I have to admit that some of the persecution bothered me at first, because my flesh was not completely dead yet. But I learned not to bow to the opinions of others, but to go with God. I knew that God would keep me and take care of me, because I was seeking Him first above all these other things that the world deemed important. God was most important to me.

At times, I would pray all night. Some people may say, "Oh, you are just exaggerating." No! That is the way it was. I was persistent. After more than a year of praying, I walked into my bedroom one day and felt the presence of God. When you have walked your floor for that long with absolutely no feelings, you will come to recognize that it is God when you sense the power of His presence. I went for two or three months longer without any further response from God. I kept knocking on heaven's door to see if someone would answer.

One day, when I walked into my bedroom and shut the door, God spoke to me, saying, "Here I am. Seek no more. I have come to hear from you." When He said that, the power of God filled my room so intensely that I was thrown across the floor. All that night I shook under the mighty power of God. This is the type of experience people are seeking. They are seeking the real because they have had enough of the counterfeit. They are looking for God to show up and say, "Here I am."

When God says that, He means, "I will be with you. I will go beside you. I will strengthen you. I will help you. I will heal through you. I will speak through you. I will bless people through you."

Not too many people have paid the price to get God to visit, but He is no respecter of persons. What He did for me, He will do for you. People try to get a visitation from God through great head knowledge. They try to reach God through money or popularity. But God is not influenced by any of these things. He is simply looking for ordinary, yielded vessels. You can be that yielded vessel. All it takes is dying to your flesh and learning to walk in the Spirit.

3

DYING TO SELF

When God came into my room, we began to walk and talk as friends. I became the student, and He became my teacher. The old Roberts Liardon began to die. God began to take away the desires of my flesh and the goals I had set for my life. I was destined for college, sports, and other things I had in mind. However, as I began to yield myself as a vessel to God, He slowly reached in and pulled Roberts out. Many nights, it seemed as if He cut me wide open, and He never used any painkillers. He just reached in and grabbed something I dearly loved in the flesh or something I wanted to do in the natural.

As my flesh began to die, I felt as if I was dying a thousand deaths. I was being nailed to my own cross. I had submitted myself to my own cross, but now God was operating on me. He was taking things out of me that were hindering me from fulfilling His call for my life. It took awhile for all those things to be pulled out of me.

One day, God took me to what I call a "spiritual graveyard." Every person who means business with God must visit this place—a graveyard where the flesh is buried. I saw a coffin with several angels standing around it. As I walked closer, I looked inside and there lay Roberts Liardon. As I saw myself in that coffin, I began to cry. There lay my wife, my children, my college, my basketball career—everything I had ever wanted or planned for my life. And I was the only one who had the power to shut the coffin. Until that day, I had not known what it really meant to "see self die." I had not understood the reality of seeing self fight for survival. I had never realized how powerful self was.

I did not realize then that the most exciting and beautiful life possible cannot begin until self dies. After I shut the lid of my coffin that day, I was buried. Then I wrote on my tombstone: "Here lie the remains of Kenneth Roberts Liardon."

When I left the "graveyard," I was sad. It is quite a task to bury your own self, your own desires. I believe it is the hardest thing Christians must do in the earth, surpassing all other spiritual experiences.

When I walked away from the graveyard that day, I had died. Later, I returned to mourn my death, and a huge angel stood in front of the graveyard and said, "Those who mourn the death of self in this place will never be able to be used for the glory of God."

Once self dies and is buried, leave it there! Do not mourn the death of your flesh. Mourning your death will cause self to revive, and it will be harder for you to die to self the second time. The complete death of one's natural self—the carnal desires, thoughts, and behavior—will lead to the resurrection by the Holy Spirit of a Spirit-controlled soul. Begin living unto God and you can begin living in the spirit world. Never go back to the flesh or the realm of self.

Crucifying Self in Order to Live

Put to death, therefore, whatever belongs to your earthly nature: sexual immorality, impurity, lust, evil desires and greed, which is idolatry. Because of these, the wrath of God is coming. You used to walk in these ways, in the life you once lived. But now you must rid yourselves of all such things as these: anger, rage, malice, slander, and filthy language from

your lips. Do not lie to each other, since you have taken off your
old self with its practices and have put on the new self, which
is being renewed in knowledge in the image of its Creator.

(Colossians 3:5–10 NIV)

The first step in living in the realm of the Holy Spirit is to die to yourself. Until you do, God will never be able to use you in the manner He desires. You cannot die to self partially and become alive unto God partially. You must get to the point where none of self and all of God Almighty remains in you. You must come to the place where you can say, with the apostle Paul:

I am crucified with Christ: nevertheless I live; yet not I, but
Christ liveth in me: and the life which I now live in the flesh
I live by the faith of the Son of God, who loved me, and gave
himself for me. (Galatians 2:20)

We are not to be ruled by the flesh; we are to be ruled by the Holy Spirit.

So then, brethren, we are debtors, but not to the flesh—we are
not obligated to our carnal nature—to live [a life ruled by the
standards set up by the dictates] of the flesh.

(Romans 8:12 AMP)

The flesh didn't cause the new birth or bring Christ to the earth. The Spirit of God brought Christ to the earth. The Spirit of God raised Jesus from the dead, and that same Holy Spirit lives in you. Yield yourself to Him.

Many believers yield themselves to the flesh rather than the Holy Spirit and then ask, "Why are my words powerless when I stand to preach? Why doesn't anything happen when I witness to people about Jesus Christ?"

When I tell people of the necessity to die to self and yield that self to the Holy Spirit they often laugh, mock, criticize, and persecute. They don't seem to realize this is the very truth that will set them free.

I believe that if the glory of God came into some churches and homes, His presence would cause the physical deaths of some people because the presence of God will not mix with willful, rebellious sin. His presence causes a reaction, an explosion called "judgment and death."

Do you remember what happened to Ananias and Sapphira in the book of Acts? It was not the presence of the apostles that caused them to fall dead when they sinned. No, they fell dead instantly when they lied in the presence of the Holy Spirit. They consciously sinned in the presence of God's glory. Willful sin and God's glory never mix.

Although Peter gave them the choice to repent, Ananias and Sapphira chose to commit spiritual suicide. If the glory of God came in the way some Christians pray for it, many more would die, also. God is not a murderer, but He does expect us to live in the light of what we know.

Until you die to self, you cannot live unto righteousness.

For if you live according to [the dictates of] the flesh you will surely die. But if through the power of the (Holy) Spirit you are habitually putting to death—making extinct, deadening—the [evil] deeds prompted by the body, you shall (really and genuinely) live forever. (Romans 8:13 AMP)

Every person is faced with the decision or choice of keeping the flesh alive or dying to self. Many people do not want what I am talking about. People who mean business with God want the presence of God without limitation or boundaries, but many are not willing to pay the price to get it.

Every person has to pay a price to step into the fullness of God's presence. Your grandma cannot pay the price for you. Your mom, dad, brothers, sisters, aunts, uncles, or cousins cannot pay the price for you. Your pastor cannot pay the price for you. You must die on your own cross.

I will admit it is a lonely road to that cross. It is a lonely death on that tree, and it is a lonely funeral. But the glory of the death and burial of self will cause a resurrection to new life. That resurrection is what multitudes of people are looking for today. The key is that *you must crucify the flesh so you can live by the Spirit.*

Esther's Cross Experience

Esther faced a "cross" experience when she had to choose whether to risk her life for the preservation of her people, the Jews, when they lived in exile. No one could approach the king unless he summoned them. Esther made the choice to risk her life and stand in the gap for her people. If the king did not hold out his golden scepter to her as she approached, the law stated that she must die.

And Mordecai told him of all that had happened unto him, and of the sum of money that Haman had promised to pay to the king's treasuries for the Jews, to destroy them. Also he gave him the copy of the writing of the decree that was given at Shushan to destroy them, to shew it unto Esther, and to declare it unto her, and to charge her that she should go in unto the king, to make supplication unto him, and to make request before him for her people. And Hatach came and told Esther the words of Mordecai. Again Esther spake unto Hatach, and gave him commandment unto Mordecai; all the king's servants, and the people of the king's provinces, do know, that whosoever, whether man or woman, shall come unto the king into the inner court, who is not called, there is one law

*of his to put him to death, except such to whom the king shall
hold out the golden sceptre, that he may live: but I have not
been called to come in unto the king these thirty days. And
they told to Mordecai Esther's words. Then Mordecai commanded to answer Esther, Think not with thyself that thou
shalt escape in the kings house, more than all the Jews. For if
thou altogether holdest thy peace at this time, then shall there
enlargement and deliverance arise to the Jews from another
place; but thou and thy fathers house shall be destroyed: and
who knoweth whether thou art come to the kingdom for such
a time as this? Then Esther bade them return Mordecai this
answer, Go, gather together all the Jews that are present in
Shushan, and fast ye for me, and neither eat nor drink three
days, night or day: I also and my maidens will fast likewise;
and so will I go in unto the king, which is not according to the
law: and if I perish, I perish.* [To make such a statement,
your flesh must be crucified!] *So Mordecai went his way,
and did according to all that Esther had commanded him.*

(Esther 4:7–17)

Esther obtained favor in the sight of the king; and because of
her willingness to jeopardize her own life—to lay aside her flesh
and what the natural realm seemed to dictate— a great victory
was obtained for her people. (See Esther 8.)

Dying to self means obeying God at any cost. Esther did that.
Is your flesh dead enough that you would risk your life to save
others?

Daniel's Cross Experience

*It pleased Darius to set over the kingdom an hundred and
twenty princes, which should be over the whole kingdom; and*

over these three presidents; of whom Daniel was first: that the princes might give accounts unto them, and the king should have no damage. Then this Daniel was preferred above the presidents and princes, because an excellent spirit was in him; and the king thought to set him over the whole realm. Then the presidents and princes sought to find occasion against Daniel concerning the kingdom; but they could find none occasion nor fault; forasmuch as he was faithful, neither was there any error or fault found in him. (Daniel 6:1–4)

No fault could be found in Daniel. He had an excellent spirit. Daniel did not bow to the flesh or to what the natural realm would dictate. Like I said earlier, when you follow after God, there will be those who are quick to criticize and persecute you. Daniel was no different, and his enemies at court knew they could find no fault in Daniel unless they could set up a situation where he would have to disobey the law of his God or the law of the king.

Knowing Daniel would not disobey his God, the dignitaries of the king prepared a decree for King Darius to sign which prohibited any person from praying to any man or god for thirty days. Their petitions were to be routed only to King Darius. The king signed the decree stating that any person who violated the decree was to be cast into the den of lions to be devoured.

All the presidents of the kingdom, the governors, and the princes, the counsellors, and the captains, have consulted together to establish a royal statute, and to make a firm decree, that whosoever shall ask a petition of any God or man for thirty days, save of thee, O king, he shall be cast into the den of lions. Now, O king, establish the decree, and sign the writing, that it be not changed, according to the law of the Medes and Persians, which altereth not. Wherefore King Darius signed the writing and the decree. Now when Daniel knew that the writing was signed, he went into his house; and his windows being open in his chamber toward Jerusalem, he kneeled upon his knees three times a day, and prayed, and gave thanks before his God, as he did aforetime. Then these men assembled, and found Daniel praying and making supplication before his God. (Daniel 6:7–11)

His enemies meant the decree to come against Daniel, a child of God. But God makes a way of escape for His own. Before deliverance came, however, Daniel had to make a choice not to cater to his flesh. He knew his God and his God knew him. Daniel knew that God's laws are higher than man's laws. He knew he could not compromise and bow to human decree when it came against God's law. Daniel took his stand. He faced his cross. He would not bow.

Daniel was cast into the den of lions for violating the decree, but because he honored God and would not bow to man, he emerged unharmed the next day. Daniel said to the king:

My God hath sent his angel, and hath shut the lions' mouths, that they have not hurt me: forasmuch as before him innocency was found in me; and also before thee, O king, have I done no hurt. Then was the king exceedingly glad for him, and commanded that they should take Daniel up out of the den. So Daniel was taken up out of the den, and no manner of hurt was found upon him, because he believed in his God. (Daniel 6:22–23)

When you will not bow to the flesh, the natural realm, or to man's decrees when they violate God's laws, great strides are made for the kingdom of God and great glory is given unto God.

Then King Darius wrote unto all people, nations, and languages, that dwell in all the earth; Peace be multiplied unto you. I make a decree, That in every dominion of my kingdom men tremble and fear before the God of Daniel: for he is the living God, and steadfast for ever, and his kingdom that which shall not be destroyed, and his dominion shall be even unto the end.   (Daniel 6:25–26)

As you examine the lives of both Old Testament prophets and New Testament figures, you will find that those who remained steadfast—not compromising God s laws and not bowing to the flesh nor to the dictates of the natural realm—achieved great accomplishments for the kingdom of God. Men and women have always come through challenges as heroes when they refused to disobey God, even at the risk of losing their own lives.

Are you willing to pay that kind of price to serve God? If not, then your flesh needs to die some more! The resurrection power of God will not flow through your life until there is death to self.

4

LIVING IN THE REALM
OF THE SPIRIT

The spirit world is an unknown realm to many Christians. Others live every day of their lives there, and they are more conscious of the spirit world than of the place called earth. Those who operate in the flesh do not understand. They look at those who have paid the price to live in the spirit world and call them "weird," "fanatic," or "in error."

However, one thing the critics cannot outdo is the miracles of those who live in the realm of the spirit. Neither can they outdo the Holy Spirit sermons they preach!

The Word of God says,

For as many as are led by the Spirit of God, they are the sons of God. For ye have not received the spirit of bondage again to fear; but ye have received the Spirit of adoption, whereby we cry, Abba, Father. The Spirit itself beareth witness with our spirit, that we are the children of God: and if children, then heirs; heirs of God, and joint-heirs with Christ; if so be that we suffer with him, that we may be also glorified together.
(Romans 8:14–17)

I once attended an overseas pastors' conference where I heard nice words spoken. The ministers there acted very friendly. They seemed glad I was there, although I knew some of them wanted money from me while others wanted the same kind of anointing I have. As I glanced around the room, it became obvious which pastors were in the process of dying to self, which had already died to self, and which were very much alive to themselves.

The churches pastored by those who had died to self were flourishing—exploding with growth and power and experiencing a great outpouring of God's Spirit. The words of these pastors carried weight. When they walked into a room or down a hallway, they commanded a subconscious respect from those about them.

Then I looked at some of those who had not died to themselves and discerned the criticism of their hearts. The Spirit of God spoke in this meeting, but by a vote of men's minds (the flesh, or soul), they delayed acting in obedience to Him. The Holy Spirit then spoke to me, "Shake the dust from your shoes. Leave them to themselves, for I am now through with them."

The Church Is at a Crossroads

I believe the body of Christ is standing at a crossroads today. If we do not make a decision to obey the Word of the Lord, tomorrow may be too late. This age is coming to a divine conclusion and when it closes, where will you be standing? Will you be standing in the flesh? Will you be standing in the midst of your crumbling world, crying and attempting to put it back together? Or will you be found searching for gold, silver, and the riches of this world? Where will you be in your relationship with God? Are you serious about the kingdom of God? Do you want to be friends with God and have an intimate relationship with Him? Do you want God to walk and talk with you everywhere you go?

If so, you must pick up your own cross and nail yourself to that tree. You must go to that graveyard and bury your flesh. You must close your coffin even though your flesh screams for survival. You must help the angels put the soil on top of your coffin. You must write your own epitaph, leave your grave, and shake the dust from your feet as you depart from that graveyard. You must leave the graveyard with your head held high and your shoulders back, ready to face a dying humanity.

People who change the course of history have died to their flesh. They do not minister only as human bodies of flesh; they minister as yielded vessels through whom the Lord Jesus Christ Himself speaks, delivers, and heals.

You may be dead to self, but you are alive with the presence of God within you. When you walk out onto a platform to minister, or when you walk into a place of business, you do not walk in as yourself but as a representative of Jesus Christ, the King of Kings and Lord of Lords. No one can look on a person who has died to self and come alive unto God without coming into contact with the truth of the gospel.

When people have died to self and Jesus walks and talks through them, they act right, talk right, look right, and walk right. When someone like that walks into a place, other people will comment, "There is something different about you." That is what the world is searching for.

The late Kathryn Kuhlman, one of the world's greatest evangelists, said that when she was backstage getting ready to go out before the people, she died a thousand deaths. She would say, "I know better than anyone else that Kathryn Kuhlman has nothing to do with what happens here today. It is not me. I have no healing power. I have no saving power. It is not my touch that will do it; it is His touch."

The world needs to see a Christian who is absolutely dead to self so the Jesus inside shines through. Criticism cannot hurt a dead person. You can walk up to a person whose flesh is dead and hit them, but they will not even respond. God uses that kind of person today.

Jesus also died to self before He died on the cross so that God could use Him. We must give ourselves up so God can use us. When I walk through a prayer line and see the hurting, the sick, and the possessed, I know my hands cannot heal them or set them free. I have no power of myself and neither do you. But as yielded vessels, the power of the Holy Spirit will freely flow through us to heal the sick, to bind up the brokenhearted, and to set the captives free. (See Luke 4:18.)

Yieldedness Impresses God

Your worldly achievements do not impress God, but your yieldedness does. The secret of understanding the Holy Spirit and allowing Him to flow in your life is yielding yourself to Him. It is not half of you and half of the Holy Spirit. The Holy Spirit does not take orders from men. He does not work with formulas. He gives the orders, and we obey. As you yield yourself completely to Him, He will flow through you.

I teach a class called "God's Generals" to Bible school students, which includes a discussion of the successes and failures of famous preachers of the past. I go through their lives in great detail and students always ask, "What caused these men and women to have such a great anointing?"

How could Smith Wigglesworth kick a crippled child from the stage into the congregation in Bradford, England, while the parents and the congregation looked on, paralyzed with fear and anxiety—yet the child landed on both feet and was made totally whole by the power of God? God works in unusual ways. Sometimes God's ways may seem strange, but the Bible says that God's ways are strange sometimes! For example, in Luke, chapter

5, when the palsied man is let down through a hole in the roof by his friends and Jesus heals him, the Word of God tells us,

> And they were all amazed, and they glorified God, and were filled with fear, saying, We have seen **strange** things to day.
> (Luke 5:26)

When the supernatural power of God is allowed to flow freely through an obedient, faithful believer, we will often see some strange occurrences!

Charles G. Finney was perhaps the greatest revivalist since the days of the apostle Paul. A very high percentage of his converts remained true to God. When Finney s horse and buggy came within two or three miles of a town, the convicting power of the Holy Spirit would hit the entire town. Revival hit the place even before he reached the outskirts!

Aimee Semple McPherson built a massive building, Angelus Temple in Los Angeles, at a cost of millions of dollars during the Great Depression. She preached twenty-one times a week. Everywhere she went, people packed the buildings and many had to be turned away. Her name was featured at least six times a week on the front page of the *Los Angeles Times*. She was the first woman to have a Christian radio station.

When Sister McPherson went into a town, she would take it for God. She did not pray long prayers or preach long sermons, but when she walked out onto the stage to preach, the power of God fell. People were healed as she preached the Word. She would have what she called "stretcher days." She would announce over her radio station that all who wanted to leave their stretchers should come to Angelus Temple on such and such a day. She would add, "You don't have to be saved. Just get here and you'll get healed. Then you'll want to get saved."

She would preach a short sermon, then say, "It is time for you to get up off your stretchers." People got up as she spoke, healed by the power of God. A man who had no eyeballs, just empty eye sockets, went to one of her meetings. Sister McPherson prayed for him, and a creative miracle occurred— God created two brand-new eyeballs in the empty sockets.

When you relate these miracles to Bible school students, they want to know how they can have that same kind of power. *That power is available to anyone who will pay the price to receive it.* People like Aimee Semple McPherson were not special people. They were ordinary people who had so completely died to self that Christ could live in and through them, bringing great glory to God. They were simply yielded vessels operating through the power of the Holy Spirit.

They were not gold or silver vessels. Gold and silver vessels only want to go to men in high places. Gold and silver vessels want some of the attention, glamour, and glory. However, they usually have little or no power. All they are is a shell.

God looks for those who have given up all of self. He is looking for those who will yield entirely to Him for service. I believe that when this type of yieldedness happens in the church as a whole, we will begin to see the greatest outpouring of the Holy Spirit ever witnessed.

Selfishness Gives Off a Stench

I never realized the importance of what happened to me when my flesh was crucified until I began traveling across the earth.

In the spirit realm, I sometimes notice a stench about some believers and Christian leaders. It is a stench that comes from people who have not died to themselves. They are the ones who are not concerned about lifting up Jesus. Instead, they are thinking, *What about me? Where do I fit in? What is in this for me? If I cannot be in the limelight, I do not want to be a part of it.*

That is a stench to God! The odor comes from a disease called selfishness. If you are fighting symptoms of this disease, repent quickly. Humble yourself before God. Refuse to let the spotlight be on anyone except Jesus Christ. You may say, "Yes, but I have such and such talent and ability that I need to use for His kingdom." You're right. Every talent and ability you have, God has placed within you and they should be used for His kingdom—but only to bring glory and honor to Jesus, not yourself. Do an attitude check on yourself regularly. Make sure that in everything you do and say, you do as unto the Lord and not as unto yourself or unto men. (See Colossians 3:17, 23.) This is how you will see the Holy Spirit s power manifested in your life.

The Bible gives us clear guidelines about what our focus and motivation should be:

> *Humble yourselves in the sight of the Lord, and he shall lift you up.*   (James 4:10)

> *And whosoever shall exalt himself shall be abased; and he that shall humble himself shall be exalted.*   (Matthew 23:12)

God will not move with His power and with a manifestation of His presence until you have given up all of the things that have held you in bondage. The price each person must pay will be different, but there will be some similarities.

Where are the Kathryn Kuhlmans, the Aimee McPhersons, the Smith Wiggleworths, the John G. Lakes, the E. W. Kenyons, the George Jeffreyses, the Martin Luthers, the John Wesleys, the George Whitefields, and the John Alexander Dowies of today? God wants people who are "sold out" to Him to work for the kingdom. God goes to and fro throughout the whole earth looking for them, and He desires to show Himself strong in their behalf.

Many Bible school students have heard me preach this sermon, only to let it go in one ear and out the other. Some leave school, go into the ministry, and come back demolished a few months later, because they have not crucified the flesh.

I want you to understand the importance of nailing yourself to your cross—the importance of dying to self—the importance of crying out to God with your whole heart, "Thy will be done; not mine, but Thine be done." That is the crossroads at which the church stands today.

Let the weights of this world fall away, including those friends who do not desire the things of the kingdom of God. Do not seek the spectacular. Too many Christians today want a fast-flying healing evangelist who can get them healed in five minutes. They want the pastor to carry the entire church into the glory of God. They want to ride with God, but they do not want to pay the fare.

I believe that since we live in the last days, we will begin to see more and more of God's power manifested in this earth. Nothing will be able to stop this great outpouring of the Holy Spirit. The gates of hell cannot prevail against what is happening in our midst. No man, no organization, no government, and no natural disaster can stop this which God has begun.

A Time for "Mighty Men"

God is raising up "mighty men" in this hour—those men and women who know what it is to fight on the devil's territory. They know what it is to get behind the lines of battle. They are the ones coming on the scene to shake the church and demand action in the pews. I say, "Let the church shake!"

The prophets of almighty God are coming out of obscurity. They are emerging with messages that will stir the hearts of men and women as never before. Their messages will cause governments to shake. Their messages will bring godly fear upon those who hear them. They will speak with boldness. They will not simply present messages with steps one, two, and three. They will speak boldly about having godly lifestyles. They will speak on prayer lives. They will speak out against sin. They will speak out against the things of the world that have crept into our churches, such as gossip, hate, idolatry, and sexual immorality. I believe God is going to speak to His church as never before.

Those who shake the earth for God will be those who are dead to self. They will know how to ascend to the throne of God and get plans for the battle. They will not wait for the enemy to attack. They are already invading enemy territory.

It is time for the church to take the kingdom of darkness by force. It is time for people in the pews to stand up and let their voices sound out among the nations. It is time for both young and old to join hands with God and let the glory of God manifest throughout the whole earth. It is time for the earth to know that God demands holiness and righteousness.

God has rules and regulations which we must observe in our daily lives. Jesus said:

A new commandment I give unto you, That ye love one another; as I have loved you, that ye also love one another.

(John 13:34)

If you walk in love, you will not sin. If you walk in love, you will live right. You will talk right. You will be right. However, if you say you are walking in love, sin on Saturday night, and show up in church as "holy" on Sunday morning, God does not agree with you.

You cannot get in the pulpit and preach a Holy Spirit sermon when you have sinned on Saturday night with your next-door neighbor's wife. You cannot preach a Holy Spirit sermon unless things are right in your life.

The church will receive correction because God loves the church. Many churches have gone without correction far too long. Any time you let a child go without correction, they will get into more trouble. Many congregations are in chaos because preachers, pastors, and evangelists have not spoken the truth as God spoke it to them. They have held back from proclaiming the truth because of people who are influential through finances or popularity. We must be like Jeremiah and Ezekiel. When the Lord says, "Speak," we must speak!

God no longer asks people to die to self; He commands it. He no longer asks people to live in holiness; He commands it. We have no time to play games anymore because the church age is coming to a close.

When time stops, wherever you are found is where you will be judged. If you have died to self, you will be in that special spot that God has ordained for you. Nothing can stop you if you live and abide in the presence of the Almightly!

SPIRITUAL TIMING

Discerning Seasons of Change
in the Realm of the Spirit

By Roberts Liardon

CONTENTS

1

TIME CAN
BE YOUR FRIEND

*That he no longer should live the rest of his time in the flesh
to the lusts of men, but to the will of God.*
—1 Peter 4:2

We need to understand, as the body of Christ, that God has a perspective from which every arena of our lives operates, whether individually or corporately. It's called "time." From the operation of that one word, lives can move forward with God or stumble. Nations can advance spiritually or regress. It all depends upon our understanding and cooperation with the timing of God.

One of the greatest needs Christians have involves understanding and operating within God's spiritual timing. As soon as we are born again, the sensitivity to the timing of God should operate in our lives. Every moment from that point forward is meant to be lived according to the will of the Father.

The world has made an attempt to harness time. They have created time management seminars and have tried to teach millions how to save time and use it more effectively. I am not against time management by any means, but some have become so time consumed, they have allowed their values to deteriorate as long as it saves some time.

Earth time usually means "rush." We have fast-food, rush-hour traffic, instant this and instant that. People in the natural fight with time. It frustrates them and produces anger. They don't like the pace of it. They either want things to slow down or to speed up. To the world, time is an enemy. Time becomes our friend in the spirit realm. People who live in the Spirit know how to work and walk with time.

God introduced His timing to us from the very first: *"In the beginning God created the heaven and the earth"* (Genesis 1:1).

That first verse in the Bible introduces us to God's timing. Everything He did was based on timing. When He created the universe, He made each part of it on a certain day, at a certain time. He formed every part of the galaxy to operate in His timing. First, He created the earth and everything surrounding it. Then, God created all of the plants, fish, animals, and birds. Finally, in His perfect timing, He created man. At this point, all of God's creation walked harmoniously with Him.

But in Genesis 3, when Adam and Eve sinned and ate of the forbidden fruit, they fell from the grace of God and began operating out of their own timing. They lost their ability to hear and follow God without a special endowment from heaven. They no longer had the ability to operate in God's timing on their own. Every generation since then has seen only trials and troubles unless God has intervened.

All through the Old Testament days, God gave information to the people concerning Himself through the prophets. He still provided them with the ability to know Him and serve Him. The understanding of spiritual times, even in those days, came from being committed to God.

One of the things that Jesus came and produced for us at Calvary was the ability to perceive and regain the correct timing of God. By receiving His redemption and walking in the Spirit, we can fine-tune our spirits to know when to be in the right place at the right time. God builds His character within us so that our decisions can line up with His will, decisions that will position us strategically in the proper season.

When you live in the Spirit, time is lovely. Time is a blessing. Spirit-filled people can walk in step with God and work the works of God without stress or strain. They understand God's timing and that time is on their side. Time means stability and nurturing. Time matures and heals. It brings understanding and abilities. Time expands and deepens our insight. When we understand God's timing, we walk with patience. As a result, we have the ability to possess our whole man—physically, emotionally, and spiritually.

Walking securely in the timing of God alleviates all fear and doubt. Godly timing produces courage, boldness, security, and strength.

God's clock is always ticking but does not resemble the human clock. If we follow the human clock, many would say we're about to run out of time.

> *Why, seeing times are not hidden from the Almighty, do they that know him not see his days?* (Job 24:1)

Job is the oldest book in the Bible. By reading the statement he made, we can see the wisdom and understanding Job had. He lived long before Moses came on the scene, and still he knew that those who truly know God know His ways and His timing.

Life in the spirit realm has a timing to it just as life in the natural realm. If you stay close to the Lord, you will be able to move according to His seasons. It is important for us to follow the Holy Spirit's leading. We must learn that it's not always right to move into action just because it seems like the thing to do. This kind of obedience only comes from prayer and intercession. Prayer alerts your spirit to the commands of heaven. It causes your spirit man to take precedence over your mind, resulting in the right action at the right time.

If you will walk strongly in the Spirit, you will be able to move according to God's clock in everything you do. You will know how much time to spend with certain people, when to build relationships, when to speak, and when to withhold. You will know when to move out on the plan of God for your family, your church, your community, and your nation.

> *And he cometh the third time, and saith unto them, Sleep on now, and take your rest: it is enough, the hour is come; behold, the Son of man is betrayed into the hands of sinners. Rise up, let us go; lo, he that betrayeth me is at hand.*
>
> (Mark 14:41–42)

Jesus knew the time had come to fulfill the greatest work ever to be done—the redemption for all mankind at Calvary.

You don't have to miss the correct timing of God in your life. Some people miss the accurate time to enter the ministry. They know God has called, but their time is not yet come because of preparation purposes, and they launch out too soon. Many have aborted their entire ministries because they gave God no time to properly equip them to handle the trouble they encountered.

> *A wise man's heart discerneth both time and judgment.*
>
> (Ecclesiastes 8:5)

We must be able to know when to go and when to stay, when to speak and when to remain silent. It is my goal to accurately hit the timing of God so heaven can reap the benefit of a full and bountiful harvest. It is the will of God that we not only be sensitive to the leadings of the Holy Spirit, but that we operate effectively in them. Time is designed by God to be one of our dearest friends.

2

DISCERNING TIMES AND SEASONS

And he said also to the people, When ye see a cloud rise out of the west, straightway ye say, There cometh a shower; and so it is. And when ye see the south wind blow, ye say, There will be heat; and it cometh to pass. Ye hypocrites, ye can discern the face of the sky and of the earth; but how is it that ye do not discern this time?
—Luke 12:54–56

If we did not understand natural times and seasons, we might go out in the dead of winter in T-shirts and shorts and freeze to death. On the other hand, we might go outside in the tropics during the summer wearing overcoats and thermal underwear and have heatstroke!

Jesus addressed this spiritual principle to His disciples, the ever-present Pharisees, and "an innumerable multitude of people" on this particular day in Galilee. (See Luke 12:1.) He was fervent in His illustration and did not give His listeners any excuse for ignorance but called them hypocrites. That was a very bold statement!

Jesus' implication was that His hearers should have known from Old Testament Scripture that they were living in the time of the Messiah. He did not confine His remarks, as He sometimes did, just to His disciples or to a small crowd—this was an innumerable multitude whom He chastised.

I believe that if Jesus were walking on the earth today and the church could see Him with natural eyes, He would be saying something similar to many of us. He not only wants, but expects, the faithful to discern spiritual times.

We live in a new day, a new spiritual time. When Jesus said, *"Let the dead bury their dead"* (Luke 9:60), He meant, "Let the past be the past." You cannot make spiritual progress if you never look beyond past moves of God any more than you can have growth in your natural life while living in the past.

Jesus said to the multitudes that day in Galilee, "How is it that you know all about the natural side of life, but you cannot tell what times you are in on the spiritual side?" God does not live in the past. It is always *today* with the Lord. He lives in the now. The greatest results you will have in your life and ministry will come when you walk in the spiritual time in which you are living—when you walk in God's present anointing.

We are to learn from the past, but we are not to live there. We are to live in the present and look to the future. Christians must learn to think in the now, or we will not see God's glory as we should, nor be able to move with Him when He moves. Many churches cherish a time in the past so much that they build a memorial to it in their minds and live there. The best way to respect the past is to build on it for the future.

The great men and women of the church's past would be the first to push us on out today. Those people who laid the path on which we walk would not be happy to think the church was living on past glories of what God accomplished through them.

Of course, we need to honor past men and women of God. We need to appreciate and learn from what they accomplished for

God's kingdom. But we cannot live, or move, or have our being in what they did, only in God. The past reputation of the church, no matter how great, is not the rock on which we are to stand. To receive today's blessing, we must move in what He is doing today.

It is not the season to act like we are about to leave the earth. It is the season to reap the harvest. It is the season to hear from heaven so we can reap the full potential of souls in all the earth. It is the season to declare the works of God in the nations. It is the time for the church to regain their sensitivity to repentance.

The trumpet has not yet sounded and we are not in a season to put on the wedding gown. We are betrothed, but we are still wearing army clothes. Wearing a wedding gown in a season of war and harvest makes you stand out as an easy target for the enemy. We must set ourselves to hear accurately what the Spirit of the Lord is doing in the earth today. If Jesus comes back tomorrow, we need Him to find us doing the work of the ministry, not sitting around waiting for something to happen.

The subject of warfare should not make you nervous. Those who do not understand the season of transition get very touchy about spiritual warfare. They do not understand that a time of transition, a day of visitation from the Lord, always means spiritual warfare. Hard work always comes before the harvest.

In Jesus' day, Satan himself came to war against the Messiah. It was a time of transition. Demons were stirred up everywhere Jesus went. He cast them out, taught His disciples to cast them out, and then made deliverance part of the Great Commission—His final instructions of war to His "soldiers." (See Mark 16:15-18.)

Revival is in progress worldwide, but God means it for the church, not for sinners. Revival means "restoration" and you cannot restore something that has never been. The body of Christ always needs refreshing and restoration before great moves of evangelism and harvest. God uses those times to prepare the "soil" in our hearts before He gathers in the lost.

Revival must not be confused with *evangelism*. God revives local churches, then they go out and evangelize, gathering in the harvest. Evangelism is the offspring of a church whose heart has been revived. The time of preparation for God's move has been going on for several years now.

If you are living in the past while hearing the message for today, the message will not make any sense to you. You may think it is false or confusing, and you will probably want to come against it—just as the Pharisees did in Jesus' day. They were trying to live in the past glory of Israel. They had built a memorial to Moses and the Law and were looking backward instead of forward to the New Covenant whose time had come.

You can choose to live in any time zone you want to live as a Christian. You have the choice to live in the past, if you so desire. You have the opportunity to sit and wait for the coming of the Lord, if you so decide. But to live on the cutting edge and to be fully alive with the Spirit of God is to move with what God is doing in the earth right now—today.

The Pharisees did not hear the message proclaimed in their day. Although they were to lead the people, they did not know the season and timing of God. However, the demons knew the spiritual time. When Jesus cast a legion of demons out of a "crazy" man, the demons spoke to him of that time:

> *And, behold, they cried out, saying, What have we to do with thee, Jesus, thou Son of God? art thou come hither to torment us before the time?* (Matthew 8:29)

You see, even demons are aware that God has a time to do certain things. They knew it was not His time for them to be shut up forever in the lake of fire.

Demons who operate in the low, carnal area are not very intelligent. They do not think or reason. However, those workers for Satan who are part of his hierarchy—the principalities, powers, and rulers of darkness—know what is going on with the kingdom of God. (See Ephesians 6:12.) If the devil and his angels and demons know about time, then certainly the body of Christ should set themselves to know.

New Testament Transition

The three years that covered the ministry of John the Baptist and Jesus were a time of major transition from the Old Covenant to the New Covenant. That is why Jesus' first and only message in His hometown of Nazareth made a clear statement of the spiritual season they were in.

> *And he came to Nazareth, where he had been brought up: and, as his custom was, he went into the synagogue on the sabbath day, and stood up for to read.* (Luke 4:16)

Jesus was accustomed to going into the synagogue and reading the text for the day. The people knew Him. This was not the first time He had read the Scripture. In verse 17, it says they gave Him the book of Isaiah to read.

God arranges situations in His timing, and it is important that we do not get in His way. God had appointed this very day for Jesus to declare to His family and neighbors who He was. In God's time, Jesus read from the prophetic book of Isaiah. Because they had known Jesus all of His life, they got the first chance to hear that the day of visitation was at hand. Many times, when God sends a person out, He sends them first to their family and friends.

Jesus, sensitive in His spirit, followed God's timing, although He must have known it would make the religious crowd angry. We must follow His example today.

> *The Spirit of the Lord is upon me, because he hath anointed me to preach the gospel to the poor; he hath sent me to heal the brokenhearted, to preach deliverance to the captives, and recovering of sight to the blind, to set at liberty them that are bruised, to preach the acceptable year of the Lord....And he began to say unto them, This day is this scripture fulfilled in your ears.*   (Luke 4:18–19, 21)

"The acceptable year of the Lord" explicitly stated the time on God's clock. Those words prophesied the coming Messiah and the listeners knew it. But they missed their day of visitation because they clung to the past time of God. They had grown comfortable in the past they understood.

Jesus tried to tell them, "These things were foretold for a certain day. Now that day has arrived. It is today." But they would not hear. They could not sense the appointed time and season of God.

John the Baptist also proclaimed the timing of God in that day.

> *And saying, Repent ye: for the kingdom of heaven is at hand....I indeed baptize you with water unto repentance: but he that cometh after me is mightier than I, whose shoes I am not worthy to bear: he shall baptize you with the Holy Ghost, and with fire.*   (Matthew 3:2, 11)

Then, the very next day, he saw Jesus and said:

> *This is he of whom I said, After me cometh a man which is preferred before me: for he was before me.*   (John 1:30)

After he baptized Jesus, John knew Jesus was the Son of God when the Holy Spirit descended on Him in the form of a dove. God gave that sign to acknowledge the Son of God. (See John 1:31–34.)

John knew that he had a work to fulfill before Jesus would come. He knew his ministry was going to be short, and he did not try to minister longer than God needed him to. When Jesus showed up, John said, *"He must increase, but I must decrease"* (John 3:30).

John the Baptist did not fight to stay in charge of the hour. He let Jesus take over. We need to know that not only do times and seasons change, but we need to know *when* they change and whether it means we are to increase or decrease.

God Changes the Times and Seasons

> *And he changeth the times and the seasons: he removeth kings, andsetteth up kings: hegiveth wisdom unto the wise, and knowledge to them that know understanding.* (Daniel 2:21)

We must become sensitive and mature enough in the spirit that when God changes the times and seasons to which we are accustomed, we do not get angry or upset. We must move with what He is doing, not against it. We cannot change times and seasons. We cannot even rearrange them. We cannot hold them still because God raises up and brings down.

When Daniel found himself in captivity in Babylon, he knew it was God's season for pruning rebellion and idolatry off His people through exile and life in a strange land. Yielding to the judgment as God told them to do would have allowed them to use the time of captivity for genuine repentance and changing of their ways. They could have been blessed in Babylon, and many were. (See Jeremiah 29:4–14.)

*Whoso keepeth the commandment shall feel no evil thing: and
a wise man's heart discerneth both time and judgment.*

(Ecclesiastes 8:5)

A wise man knows both the timing of God as well as the judgment of God. A foolish person knows neither. An immature Christian will cherish something beyond its time. A mature Christian will be joyful over change because it is according to God's will. A mature Christian knows God never brings us down—no matter how it looks on the outside. He always brings those who love and serve Him up to a better place. God's change is always for the best.

Spiritual Hunger

An important characteristic, spiritual hunger, causes God to take us from one season to another. In Jesus' day, just as in our day, many were caught up in a past time. But on the other hand, many also had a dissatisfaction in their hearts. Because of the sensitivity to the things of God, they knew, it was time for a change. There was no longer the peace of relying on the letter of the law that there had been. The desire for the Messiah to come had intensified in their hearts. The Pharisees also intensely wanted Messiah to come, but their desire came from their minds. Their "Messiah" had to fit their own scenario—not God's—so they missed Him.

Today, there is a hunger for truth—a hunger for the Word. Physical hunger is one of the most powerful drives on the earth because it directly relates to survival of the body. In the same way, spiritual hunger is one of the most powerful instincts in the spirit realm because it supports the survival of our spiritual walk.

When people are starving, they will do things that otherwise they would not do. They will eat things that in better times would not be acceptable at all. The same is true in spiritual hunger. People are hungry for the written Word and for a direct, personal word from God. They are hungry for the fullness of the fivefold offices. They are so hungry to see God move that in many places, if they are not fed, they try to fill their hunger through false prophecies and false prophets.

Some are trying to do it themselves, trying to take hold of the prophetic anointing, and they are making big mistakes.

I believe that a hunger for anything spiritual is a sign that God's time has changed. God's answer to the spiritual craving in the earth today is on its way. The truth is coming in stability and accuracy. As we continue to prepare our hearts, God will continue to mature his leaders and proclaimers. By staying in the Word of God and prayer, we will continue to sharpen our sensitivity and excel in maturity.

When you sense God changing the times and seasons of your life, don't resist Him. Change can be very exciting to those who are hungry for the Spirit of God. Don't get complacent in your time with God or too comfortable in your relationship with Him. Stay hungry for the things of God and He will keep you in His perfect timing.

3

A TIME FOR GIFTS, REVELATIONS, AND OFFICES

A man hath joy by the answer of his mouth: and a word
spoken in due season, how good is it!
—Proverbs 15:23

In this time of spiritual transition, the church should always be seeking God to find His timing. Believers and particularly those who are in ministry should find out what times and seasons they live in, for there are certain times that certain things are to be spoken. A word spoken out of season brings more confusion than blessing, but a word spoken in season brings joy and clarity.

The Lord GOD hath given me the tongue of the learned, that
I should know how to speak a word in season to him that is
weary. (Isaiah 50:4)

When we walk in the spirit, we have the ability to speak the correct words at the correct time. The right words at the right time will refresh, rearrange, and encourage those who hear. That is our purpose. The right timing of God will produce an atmosphere in which we can release the revelation inside of us. But if we speak out in the wrong timing, our words produce a counter-reaction in the hearts and minds of the people.

When a believer speaks and delivers a revelation at the right time, it spreads like wildfire. Many people speaking true words from God have gone through unnecessary persecution because the person delivering the message didn't understand the proper timing. Even a true word, given at the wrong time, can do much damage.

One thing believers must learn is how to know when a word is in season. So many just hear something and run with it, causing a negative reaction everywhere they go. Those people need an understanding of time. Just because we have a "word" doesn't mean it is to be delivered at that exact moment.

On the other hand, many believers and ministries live in frustration because they try to analyze the timing of God through public opinion, intellect, or organization. As a result, they wear themselves out physically, emotionally, and spiritually. The ministry suddenly becomes a dreaded chore, followed by disillusionment and sin. Some have even left the ministry, feeling exhausted and seared. We need to know when to move and when to rest. Faith is now, but godly results are birthed from accurate timing.

The sign of a mature Christian is his ability to walk accurately in God's timing. A young Christian is characterized by his mistakes with timing. That does not mean he is in deep trouble; it simply means he is in a learning process.

When I was learning this, I would get a message in my heart and hold it. It was so much inside of me that I would stand in front of my mirror and speak it out to myself! When you have a strong message inside of you, it is alive, almost like a baby. It is "kicking" and moving, and you want it to come forth and be born. You begin to say, "When is it going to be time?" If you are not careful, the message can become an irritation to you instead of a blessing.

But when that message inside of me came out in God's timing, it was wonderful! It went all over the country when I preached it because I hit the right time with it. Revelation must be released in accuracy of time. Everything the Holy Spirit gives you belongs in a sequence of His timing.

Unction or Emotion?

I've had prophecies for individuals that I wanted to give right then. My soul said they needed to hear it, but in my spirit I had no release to give it. So I had to wait.

We must learn the difference between emotion and unction. You do not give a word from God without the unction. An attempt to move in the Spirit by emotion will pull you out from the correct timing of God every time. Learning and operating with the unction in our spirit will keep us in step with His timing. We must speak out of the unction of spirit, not the pull of emotion.

The Greek word *charisma* means "an unguent, or a smearing with oil or a salve," and it is usually translated as some form of the word "anoint."[1] The scholars who translated the King James Version of the Bible used *"unction"* as an English translation of *charisma* only one time in the entire Bible.

> *But ye have an unction from the Holy One, and ye know all things.* (1 John 2:20)

"Unction" simply means "anointing." Do not give a prophecy to anyone unless you have the anointing from the Holy Spirit to do so. There must be a divine stirring inside of you. It is not based on an emotion. It is not a "good idea" that would make the person feel better. That unction from God literally draws it out of you,

---

1. James Strong, *The Exhaustive Concordance of the Bible* (Nashville: Abingdon, 1890), "Greek Dictionary of the New Testament," 78, #5545.

for it is the unction, or anointing, that brings the prophecy forth in power.

Sometimes I have a prophecy in my spirit, and I walk into a meeting where the people seem to be really rejoicing, praising God, and ready to receive. But there is no unction on me to give forth the word. Then I go into another meeting where it does not look as if anything is happening, and boom! There comes the prophecy.

I used to wonder why God would give it to those people and not the ones at the earlier meeting. Then I began to see that only God knows the heart and level of maturity. His prophecies are meant to begin a work immediately when they are received.

One of the fivefold offices is that of a prophet. Prophets must be very sensitive to the timing of the Holy Spirit. If they are not aware of the timing of God, they can get involved in self-inflicted or self-caused persecution by releasing and doing things without an anointing or before the proper time. Prophets are very aware of what God is doing today and in the future. Just because they have the ability to "see" what God will do doesn't mean it is time to announce it or to try to cause it to happen. It is of utmost importance that prophets remain sensitive to the timing of God.

Some time ago, I became so tired of hearing "dead" prophecies. I thought if I heard another one, I would scream. Dead prophecies are exhortations out of someone's soul. They may be heartfelt, but they are not words from God and should not be given forth as such. No matter how good they sound or how scriptural they are, there is no anointing to prophesy on those words. If people are learning how to operate in the gifts or in the prophetic office, that is one thing. But some people have given out dead prophecies for years.

The unction gives you power to speak out the word of God in a high-ranking force. It carries weight and rearranges the thoughts and the direction we walk. Our emotions say that an exhortational prophecy means "pat me," but biblical exhortation means to urge, admonish, push on, and warn.

The apostle Peter wrote that in old times, men of God spoke by the Holy Spirit, not by the will of men. (See 2 Peter 1:21.) The New Testament times or present-day times are no different. When a word is spoken in the correct timing with unction, it will come with weight, power, and force. The Holy Spirit knows the perfect time.

We must learn not to give forth a word just because an auditorium is full or the conditions seem right. It would be easy to release a word from the Lord when excitement runs high, but we must train ourselves to let the Holy Spirit lead us, not the excitement level around us. The unction within will direct us to the appointed time.

Time for Prophetic Anointing

I believe the heart and thrust of evangelism is a prophetic anointing. The greatest evangelists I have ever seen are those with the prophetic anointing. They are sensitive to the timing of God. They understand the seasons of God and the workings of the prophetic office. In fact, it is like two streams that converge together from different directions to form a mighty river. The prophetic stream and the evangelistic stream meet head on and will merge; they will not conflict.

In the latter part of 1989, the Spirit of God began to bring out of me in prayer a call for the prophetic evangelist to come into the earth, to go through the nations reaping a harvest by saying and doing what God directs. I began to see the prophetic anointing come on some evangelists, but some tended to be afraid because they were placed in arenas in which they were not accustomed.

The natural side of people always wants to understand what is happening before stepping out. However, some things you learn simply by moving out in faith.

I saw one particular evangelist move out with the prophetic anointing, and the manifestation of God was very strong because he was sensitive to the changing and timing of the Holy Spirit. As he began to preach on the glory of God, the glory of God began to manifest in the room. I believe that is characteristic of functioning in the Holy Spirit s accurate timing with a prophetic anointing. What is preached or taught will show forth as the minister steps out in faith.

As this evangelist preached, I could feel the glory of God come in the room. The stronger he preached, the stronger the glory became. His preaching was more like prophesying without saying, "Thus saith the Lord," in the middle of his sermon. He began this way: "The word of the Lord is..." then the rest of the sermon was the word of the Lord. Soon, people all over the room began to weep. They began to come down the aisles without an altar call. Some of them ran to the altar. The glory of God and the conviction of the Holy Spirit were so strong that even those already saved wanted to be saved again! It was one of the most anointed meetings I had ever been in.

I believe all of the fivefold offices are experiencing a new day with a prophetic anointing resting on all of them to a certain degree. We have prophetic pastors, prophetic teachers, and prophetic evangelists operating differently than we have been accustomed to seeing.

There have been prophetic evangelists before because God's "new thing" is usually restoration of something that has been lost or forgotten by the church. John the Baptist was one who preached under a prophetic anointing, telling of things to come and warning of judgment at the same time he called people to repentance.

The anointing was what brought conviction. Otherwise, John the Baptist was no different from other "wild men" of his day, who spent solitary time in the desert and came out preaching. His sensitivity to God's perfect timing, the presence of the Holy Spirit, and the prophetic anointing made John the Baptist different.

Timing with Praise and Worship

We have begun to see a prophetic anointing on praise and worship. Tradition is very strong in that area. Many churches have been delivered from the hymnbook but are now stuck on transparencies. Some are still at the mercy of the machine that throws lyrics onto the wall or to a certain systematic song order.

The old songs were not the problem. "Religion" had crept in through routinely singing the same old way in the flesh. The newness of the songs fooled us. Because they were fresh, we could really get involved singing them. But new songs are not a substitute for the Holy Spirit's anointing, nor are they a sure sign of it. New songs or old songs, it is the spirit in which we sing them that counts.

Some churches have set their entire congregation backwards because of the songs they sang before the message. The ministers leave frustrated because they can't understand why the people couldn't grasp what they delivered to them. The song service left the people stagnant and crusty, making it difficult to receive the full impact of the message. We need to quit holding on to something because we are comfortable with it and move out with the timing of the Spirit.

Sometimes, simple obedience will change the flow. I was scheduled to speak at a certain church one Mother's Day. Usually, I have a word or a stirring in my spirit, but I could not get anything for that particular service. Before I left for the church, I looked up Scriptures about mothers, and none of them were anointed to me. I walked into the pastor's office and said, "Pastor, I don't have anything for mothers today."

He said, "That's good because I preached about that last week."

I thought, *Hallelujah! I don't have to worry about that.* But then the real problem came—I did not know what to preach. So I said, "I'll just go by faith."

The music started and they were singing the usual charismatic/Word-Faith songs. I was being nice and preferring my brethren, being very sweet and respectful, but then the Lord said to me, "I want you to dance." So I began dancing very easily, when the Lord said, "No, no, no!"

I said, "Well, what do You want then?" He said, "I want the old combined with the new." I said, "Oh. You mean, don't 'wiggle' but *dance*." And He said, "Yes."

Now I am coming out of tradition as fast as I can, but I have to admit there is a little bit left. I am further than some people, but there are still things I am dealing with. I said, "But Lord, it's Mother's Day! Everyone is wearing flowers." I knew God was going to do a work in that place, but I also knew that everyone was dressed up with flowers pinned to their dresses, and with visitors there, no one wanted to sweat—after all, it was Mother's Day!

But when the Lord says "dance" to me, that does not mean your normal two-step. That means *dance*. When I dance, I get into it all over. I am everywhere. Well, I started to dance.

On the way up into the spirit realm, you have to fight demons, whether it is through prayer or praise and worship. Half of the front row went with me. A member of my staff also moved with me. As soon as I began to really dance, I was in a fight. It was not one of those bringing-down-the-glory dances, it was a

we-are-going-to-win dance. There was a controlling spirit domi-
nating that church and God wanted them set free.

Sometimes we get into places that we know very little about.
We must know the accurate timing of God in order to move cor-
rectly with what the Spirit of God intends to do. We were singing a
praise song full of zeal, and the atmosphere was being flooded with
the praises of the people when suddenly the musicians started to
change over to a worship song. It was not the time to move from a
praise song into a quiet, worship song. The unction was strong in
me, and I said, "Don't do it! Go back to that other song and let's
sing it some more." We went back to the first song, and people
all over the building began to enter in with us except the musicians. Because they hadn't been sensitive to the timing of God,
they remained startled that their systematic order changed. They
were trying to be nice and sweet. The Holy Spirit wanted to move
among the people, but the musicians weren't cooperating.

I finally moved over and stood right in the middle of the
instrumentalists. They looked petrified, but I kept telling them,
"Play with force! Play with force!" Finally, they hit it with force.
For two and a half hours, we sang, danced, and sweated, and that
controlling spirit came down that day. That church was set free.

The service was noisy, yet decent and in order. What most
people call "decently and in order" means organizing the Holy
Spirit out, but that's not it at all. Freedom to that church did not
come by preaching or prophesying. Freedom came by being sensitive to God's chosen way for the hour. It came to them by allowing
the Holy Spirit to do His work, and it came by the minstrel and
the dance.

We must be careful not to learn from a "system." We must
learn from the unction, or we become religious. God wants us
to move under His unction, not by performance or by "working
things up" through emotion and the flesh.

Some musicians and song leaders sing and play out of their heads only and are not sensitive to the leading of the Holy Spirit. Many of their gifts are being aborted, because they choose to operate completely in the flesh through intellect and organization. It is so sad to see a worship leader in bondage to a system.

I do not know music, but I do know how to lead praise and worship in the Spirit. At times an anointing, an unction, comes on me for those things. I must hear the timing of God in each service in which I minister. We must learn to operate from that unction, for it will lead to godly results every time.

4

PITFALLS OF
THE WRONG TIMING

King David was a man after God's own heart. (See 1 Samuel
13:14.) Yet, he is a classic example of a leader of God's people
who missed the spiritual timing of the hour. Second Samuel
11 records a tragic incident in David's life. In past years, when
I preached on that chapter, I used it as a text for a message on
sexual misconduct. However, on an airplane flying home from
Europe, the Lord prompted me to reread the story. Then He
asked me a question, "Why did David commit these sins at this
particular time?"

I began to talk to the Lord about it, and I answered Him with
my usual thought on David s misconduct with Bathsheba. He
said, "Read it again."

> And it came to pass, after the year was expired, at the time
> when kings go forth to battle, that David sent Joab, and his
> servants with him, and all Israel; and they destroyed the chil-
> dren of Ammon, and besieged Rabbah. But David tarried still
> at Jerusalem. (2 Samuel 11:1)

The Lord asked me, "What time was it?"

I said, "It was the end of the year."

The Lord said, "That is not the time I am talking about. That
is natural time. What time was it otherwise?"

I said, "That verse says it was the time when kings go forth to battle."

That was it! David missed the timing God ordained for him to follow. The sins for which he is so remembered are only the surface of a core problem—he missed God's timing.

Where was David at a time when the kings went forth into battle? Where was the king when his men were out fighting for the country and taking territory that the Lord had promised? God gave land to them, but they had to occupy it. Instead of leading the fight for the Lord, David sent his men to fight while he stayed home. This was very unusual behavior for a king.

When people do not operate in God's timing for them, they are vulnerable to the traps and temptations of the enemy. David ended up committing adultery and murder because he did not go with his men into battle, thus missing the timing of God.

Missing God's timing is as dangerous as deliberately being disobedient. David had removed himself from underneath the shelter of His wings. The same thing can happen to us to one degree or another. I believe the degree is associated with how much we are aware of His timing. He will never leave us, but we quite often walk away from Him. He is still our Father, yet we are not in the close fellowship necessary to be in tune with Him. When we are not in tune with or sensitive to the Holy Spirit, we do not hear Him as clearly when He warns us of things to come.

Hosea 4:6 speaks of God's people being destroyed through lack of knowledge. David's lack of insight, that to miss God's timing might destroy him, almost did exactly that.

Some may say, "But his main problem was not spending enough time in prayer or communion with God." Even prayer and studying the Word cannot substitute adequately for obedience and for moving out in God's direction and His time. However, what prayer and reading the Word will do is make it more likely that you will hear from God if you are out of His place or time and enable you to get back in right relationship with the Lord.

David was a strong leader, anointed and chosen by God, so how did he miss the timing of God? As I went on to study 2 Samuel, I saw some major character flaws in David at this particular point in his life.

Pride

The main root of David's problem at this time was pride. Any leader who is in true, humble authority will be with his people and not on a man-made pedestal. David placed himself on a pedestal by refusing to be in the battle with his people. After all, he was the king and he could do whatever he wanted, with whom he wanted, whenever he wanted. He could invent his own rules and regulations if he so desired. He had the money, the power, the comfort, the reputation, and the respect. The people already knew he was a great warrior. He no longer felt he had to maintain that reputation because it was firmly established.

Although God gave him these blessings, David chose at this particular time to set himself up as his own law. He chose to remain in the king's palace, comfortable and safe, rather than be with his men in battle. David did not realize that walking out from the spiritual timing of God is deadlier than any natural weapon on the battleground.

The main reason we would knowingly walk out from the correct timing of God is to get our own way. When we do not walk in the Spirit and our heart is not submitted to the will of God, the only thing left to lead us is our carnal desires.

And it came to pass in an eveningtide, that David arose from off his bed, and walked upon the roof of the kings house: and

from the roof he saw a woman washing herself; and the woman
was very beautiful to look upon.   (2 Samuel 11:2)

When we are not submitted to the timing of God, peace leaves and restlessness comes. David's mind was obviously racing with thoughts. Driven from sleep by his active mind, he got up, walked out on the roof one night, and caught a glimpse of a beautiful woman bathing. All of the men in Israel should have been out in battle. The woman was in her right to bathe, not knowing any man was left in the city.

When we are out of the will and timing of God, our mind is not on the things of heaven. David's own desire consumed him, and he became obsessed to conquer Bathsheba.

Because of his intense pride at that time, it no longer mattered to David what was right or wrong. It no longer mattered that she was another man's wife. It didn't even matter that the woman's husband was one of his most faithful servants, Uriah the Hittite. (See 2 Samuel 11:8–13.) All that mattered to David was that his desire be fulfilled, no matter what the cost.

It is sad to say that when a person comes to this point, they are usually capable of any and all sin. Their conscience is seared. I have seen friends and ministers fall because of their uncontrolled desire, and some lose that for which they have given their whole lives.

And David sent messengers, and took her; and she came
in unto him, and he lay with her; for she was purified from
her uncleanness: and she returned unto her house. And the
woman conceived, and sent and told David, and said, Iam
with child.   (2 Samuel 11:4–5)

Instead of waking up and repenting, David fell deeper into sin to cover his selfish actions. He turned into another man, one totally opposite of the character that God had exalted in him. He began to plot, scheme, and lie to cover his error. He began to betray his people and his household by pretending to be something he wasn't.

When uncontrolled desire consumes a person, normalcy leaves. It almost seems as if common sense is nowhere to be found. Extreme behavior patterns surface because the desire has become so great that the sense of right and wrong has been numbed.

Those who have reached this stage of desire will cut off association with all those around them who have a different standard. They will gather others to themselves who support their ways, some twisting Scripture and principles to do it. Uncontrolled desire has blinded them from the timing and relationship of God.

Missing God's timing as a result of selfish desire causes people to devour anything that stands in their way. When they step out of His proper timing, it means they step into every vice that can accompany the wrong. When uncontrolled desire leads a life without repentance, acts of betrayal, lying, stealing, cheating, lust, and eventually physical death can follow.

In the rest of the chapter, David attempted to deceive and flatter Uriah, the woman's husband, to go home and sleep with his wife so it would appear the baby was his. But Uriah was so faithful and trusting of David's kindness, he vowed even deeper loyalty to his country and refused to be with his wife.

Out of desperation, with no sense of right or wrong, David had Uriah sent to the front of the battle to be killed. (See 2 Samuel 11:6-24.)

Loving Comfort

David had to face another area of pride in his heart that caused him to miss the timing of God—he was *too comfortable*.

David was surrounded by people who said "yes" to whatever he dictated. Because his heart had become turned by comfort, he used those whom God had sent to him for his own gain and protection.

If you are not surrounded by those who can sharpen you like iron, you are being set up for a great fall. Many friends and ministers I have seen pad themselves inside a group of "yes men." They surround themselves with these people because it comforts them. But the problem is when they fall, those on the cutting edge cannot hear their cry for help because the "padding" is so thick from those who surround them. We cannot stay accurate if we surround ourselves with unreality. When we are too comfortable, we lose our cutting edge. Loving comfort will rob us from hitting the timing of God.

If we run from confrontation for fear that it might shake our comfort zone, then we are heading straight into defeat. Comfort zones will not always throw someone into sexual sins. Other people usually fall prey to religious spirits. They are the ones who are easily offended.

A minister once said to me, "Well, Roberts, I feel that all we need to do is just preach the gospel." Well, I believe that too, but there is more to the gospel than just giving it out. There is an accuracy in timing we must learn to hit, and character is one of the items on our checklist which teaches us accuracy.

Many who like comfort zones will not like this book. Learning to walk with God's timing means responsibility and an amount of pressure, and comfort-loving people have put aside both of those.

How does a person end up loving comfort more than God? There are several causes. One is sin in the heart:

> *For all that is in the world, the lust of the flesh, and the lust of the eyes, and the pride of life, is not of the Father, but is of the world*
> (1 John 2:16)

The Amplified Bible of the same verse says the pride of life is the *"assurance in one's own resources or in the stability of earthly things."* These are not of God, but of the world, and they will cause a person to love comfort more than the Father.

Many lose their focus when they become more comfortable with a maintenance ministry than moving with what God is doing today. We would all like to stay in certain areas, but like it or not, times and seasons all come to an end, and new ones always begin. If you get caught in the wrong time because of comfort, captivity and sin will begin to settle in.

Sometimes breaking new ground—going where people have not gone in ways that seem untraditional—can get you into trouble with your peers. Some fear that being different than other churches will hurt their church growth. Many pastors today are very selective about the things they preach. They don't want to preach anything that might be the least bit offensive to their congregations. But the fact is, the truth is often offensive and often uncomfortable.

When we read the stories of the men and women who did great exploits in the Bible, we can see by their lives they certainly did not seek comfort or security, nor did they live in comfortable, stable, and secure times. If you begin to sense God moving in a different way than you have been used to seeing, accept it. Do not reject God's calling or hold it away from you. On the other hand, test every spirit by the Word of God. It is not smart to go to the extreme and think, *Well, this is a different thing, so it must be from God!*

You may be trying to make your life fit the way you have it planned. But to move accurately in the timing of God, you have to be willing to have your plans turned upside down from the way you originally thought.

Years ago, the Lord taught me something very important that has kept me out of the comfort zone. He said, "Do not try to live your life according to what other people do." I have learned to live my life two ways: according to the timing of God and according to the calling upon my life.

On the other hand, allowing people to think you are special because of doing things God's way is also a trap of the devil to hinder you. Because I did follow God's timing and live my life differently than many others my age, people called me *unique*. I did not know how to respond to that, so I would agree that I was different. Then the Lord said to me, "You quit agreeing with a lie! You are not a unique case. That will open a door of pride if you keep saying that. Because you are walking in My time, what is happening in your life is normal. It is not unique, peculiar, nor an oddity. Your life is normal."

People who obey God are normal. People who walk in God's timing are normal. Those who do not know spiritual time and walk in the ways of the world are the ones who are different and out of step with God's way.

Other people used to tell me I was strange, and I would say, "Yes, I know, but I'm changing." After the Lord began to talk to me about that too, I had to stop agreeing. I began to say, "No, I'm not weird or strange, I'm normal. I just know how to walk in God's timing for my life."

Christians who are single particularly need to look for God's timing in connection with marriage. Loneliness and insecurity can be great pitfalls in which to miss the timing of God. Even if you know the one you are to marry, there is a correct timing. The Holy Spirit told me, "There are going to be many people in this day who will come close to aborting their callings because of trying to make things happen in the area of marriage."

Do not allow people or circumstances to put you in a box or place you in a certain slot and keep you there. Have faith that God knows what He is doing, and keep your mind under control. Do not allow your mind to move you from the time in which God has placed you.

Loving comfort puts us in danger of captivity, coming against a move of God, coming against the Word of the Lord, and coming against the brethren that might not believe exactly like we do.

A Heart for People

David had a third character flaw in 2 Samuel: his lack of heart for his people.

> Then David said unto the messenger, Thus shalt thou say unto Joab [concerning the planned death of Uriah], Let not this thing displease thee, for the sword devoureth one as well as another: make thy battle more strong against the city, and overthrow it: and encourage thou him.   (2 Samuel 11:25)

When we have a heart for people, as believers and leaders alike, we will listen to heaven and be by their side through good times and bad. David sent the people out to face the times alone because he felt superior to them at that time. But as he stayed behind, he fell into sin.

One of the saddest sights in the world is ministers who have lost a heart for people. When people lose their heart for the human race and turn that desire towards themselves, sin will devastate them. They will be absorbed by selfishness and unable to minister to others.

Throughout the Old Testament, God showed Himself strong on behalf of the prophets whose hearts were turned toward the people. Although the prophets were appalled at the sin of the people, they would rend their own garments and cry out for repentance with them, as if they had sinned themselves.

The prophet Jonah had a difficult time learning compassion for the people. He felt the people of Nineveh should get the punishment they deserved. God taught Jonah a hard lesson, and we never hear about him again. (See Jonah 1-4.)

Moses constantly considered the people over himself. Even with the great tasks he had to face, only once did he turn his heart against the people, reacting in anger and accusation. He disobeyed God, spoke what he felt, and called the people some very accurate names! But from that one, serious mistake, God did not allow him to enter the Promised Land. (See Numbers 20:1-12). God takes the people and the representation of His heart towards them very seriously.

The leader, Gideon, had a heart for the people.

> And the angel of the LORD appeared unto him, and said unto him, The LORD is with thee, thou mighty man of valour.
>
> (Judges 6:12)

Where would your heart be if the angel of the Lord appeared to you and told you the Lord was with you? Look at Gideon's heart:

> And Gideon said unto him, Oh my Lord, if the LORD be with us, why then is all this befallen us? and where be all his miracles which our fathers told us of saying, Did not the LORD bring us up from Egypt? but now the LORD hath forsaken us, and delivered us into the hands of the Midianites. (verse 13)

Gideon did not single himself out from the people. He did not stick out his chest, puff himself up, and say, "I've got it. I have arrived. Yes, I am chosen, God is with me. Stick with me and you will make it." No, he answered with his heart—his heart for the people.

> And the LORD looked upon him, and said, Go in this thy might, and thou shalt save Israel from the hand of the Midianites: have not I sent thee?   (Judges 6:14)

These words from the Lord were very significant. The might of Gideon to which the Lord referred was his *heart for the people* and *his heart for miracles*. These two ingredients added together produce a sensitivity to the correct timings of God.

The Lord went on to tell him in verse 16, that Gideon and the people would smite the enemy as *one man*. When leadership and believers have a heart for one another, a unity comes that the work of darkness cannot penetrate. The body of Christ is invincible when unified in heart.

Many verses show the heart of Jesus while He walked on the earth, but one in particular expresses how timing and a heart for the people walk hand in hand.

> Now before the feast of the passover, when Jesus knew that his hour was come that he should depart out of this world unto the Father, having loved his own which were in the world, he loved them unto the end.   (John 13:1)

Jesus knew His time to leave this world had come. But notice the last part of that verse: "having loved his own which were in the world, he loved them unto the end."

Although those closest to Him betrayed, persecuted, misrepresented, beat, and lied about Him, His heart remained fixed for the benefit of all mankind, even to His death. As a result, He triumphantly fulfilled the plan of the Father for all eternity.

Whatever God has called you to do, be it to lead or to follow, do it with a heart for people. Do not let pride or comfort prevent you from fulfilling the perfect plan of God at the perfect time. When God says, "Go," go! When God says, "Wait," then wait. Do not become impatient, but trust in the Lord and in His ways.

And being fully assured that what God had promised, He was able also to perform. Therefore also it was credited to him as righteousness. (Romans 4:21–22 NASB)

5

BLESSINGS OF
THE RIGHT TIMING

The most important thing in these last days is to find the correct timing of God in your life and walk in it.

One of the most successful stories in the Bible concerning two people who operated in the correct timing of God was Esther and Mordecai. Esther's name means "star," and as far as I am concerned, she gets one in my book.[2]

Just as we have discussed character flaws that cause one to miss God's timing, we need to take a look at some attributes that cause us to come into the right timing.

Godly Authority

In the Old Testament book of Esther, an interesting story unfolds. King Ahasuerus had just relieved Queen Vashti of her royal duties and had proclaimed the call for a new queen throughout the region. (See Esther 2:1–5.) Mordecai's uncle had died and left a daughter, Esther, whom he had taken in and raised as his own. Esther became one of the many women taken into the palace to stand before the king. (See Esther 2:7–8.)

Although she was on her own in the palace, Mordecai asked that she not reveal her kindred nor show that she was a Jew.

---

2. Strong, *The Exhaustive Concordance of the Bible* (Nashville: Abingdon, 1890), "Hebrew and Chaldee Dictionary," 15, #635.

Keeping this secret was not deceptive: it was not the time to reveal it, and Mordecai sensed it. His wisdom caused him to be exalted later on. Esther's submission to Mordecai's authority and godly advice enabled her to enter into God's correct timing, and it saved the entire Jewish nation from destruction. (See Esther 2:10–23.)

Godly authority is designed to be our protection and covering. Finding and submitting to godly authority creates a strength inside of us and gives us the added courage to walk in obedience. What we do then is ordained by God and not appointed by a friend or an idea.

In Numbers 16, Korah and those most popular in the camp took on the fatal assumption that they had as much authority over the people as Moses and Aaron did. They voiced the same murmur we hear today from those who know no better, "We are just as holy as you and we can hear God for ourselves. Who do you think you are, trying to be the leader?" (See Numbers 16:2–3.)

Every New Testament believer has the ability and the unction within to hear from God for themselves concerning themselves. But God has ordained for some to be endowed in the fivefold ministry, a ministry of leading and training the body of Christ. (See Ephesians 4:11–16.) He gave them titles—apostle, prophet, evangelist, pastor, and teacher. Their function is to mature the saints and teach them how to hear God for themselves so they will not be deceived. Jesus gave these gifts, and the responsibility and pressure that accompany them can be staggering at times. Many of those called into the five-fold ministry have never sought those gifts. The apostle Paul goes on to explain what we do once we understand the function of the five-fold ministry gifts:

> *This I say therefore, and testify in the Lord, that ye henceforth walk not as other Gentiles [or carnal ones] walk, in the vanity [emptiness] of their mind, having the understanding*

darkened, being alienated from the life of God through the ignorance that is in them, because of the blindness of their heart.   (Ephesians 4:17–18)

Do you see what Paul is saying? If we walk in our own ways, not submitted to authority, we will not know the timing of God for our lives because we will be surrounded by darkness and blindness. Being **alienated from the life of God** for the believer means not walking according to His time and season. There is abundant life when we walk with God. As a matter of fact, we cannot walk with God and be out of His timing.

We are not to put those in leadership on a pedestal, but we are to respect and honor them for teaching us and giving their lives for the ways of the Lord. By doing so and learning from their lives and ministries, it causes our hearts to be sensitive to the correct seasons of God. As a result, maturity and blessings follow us.

It is imperative that we submit ourselves to godly authority in this hour, believer and leader alike, so the Holy Spirit can accomplish His plan through us and save the nations of today.

Motives Must Be Right

After Esther was chosen to be a maiden in the palace, it was time for her to be brought before the king. The palace had a set regulation that whatever the maiden asked for or desired was to be given to her. (See Esther 2:13.) Such a vast ruling would certainly expose the generosity or lack of it in a person's heart! The remaining maidens must have asked for much, for in verse 15 we hear how Esther was different:

Now when the turn of Esther, the daughter of Abihail the uncle of Mordecai, who had taken her for his daughter, was come to go in unto the king, she required nothing but what Hegai the king's chamberlain, the keeper of the women, appointed.

(Esther 2:15)

Here is the result of a right motive:

And Esther obtained favour in the sight of all them that looked upon her.

(verse 15)

To obtain the favor of God for the nations, we must have right motives in our heart. Many people have attempted to cover their motives through flattery or deception, but the truth always comes to light. In this hour, time is speeding up because the end is drawing near. That means the works of men come to light in a quicker way—good and bad. The right motive, even when you make a mistake, will protect you and keep you sensitive to the heart of God. We need to continuously check our motives and stay tuned to the Holy Spirit.

Some time ago, I was in a meeting with pastors and teachers, and they were talking about "how everyone thinks they are prophets today." Finally, they asked me what I thought. I got bold and said, "Your motives are not right. The only reason one would be so touchy about prophets is if they are nervous for their own ministries and pastorates.

"If you talk about something happening in the church in the right spirit, there is no criticism. You can be cautious, but you will not be judgmental nor come against something God is doing or against some other person in the body. That kind of discussion with the right motive is led by the Holy Spirit. It brings truth and an earnest seeking of God's help.

"Something is wrong with the way you are talking about prophets and the restoration of that office. Remember the healing revival? Remember how many people misused the gifts? Remember the extremes that people went to—no doctors, no medicine, and so forth? Why didn't you throw out the foundational principle of healing when those errors and false manifestations began to occur?

"What about the faith movement and all of those on the fringes who got into presumption? Why didn't you throw out the faith message?

"What about prosperity and all those who misunderstood and gave money thinking they would get a new car or a new house? Why didn't you throw out the prosperity message?

"You didn't because there was still truth in the middle of error. There was a pure message from God and a revelation in there somewhere. Right now, God is restoring deliverance, intercession, and the prophetic. Yes, some imbalance is going to surface, but are you going to throw out the pureness of God's truth along with the flesh and the demonic that try to get involved? Are you going to throw the baby out with the bathwater?"

I hope they really heard what the Holy Spirit said, or those people will miss God's timing and season for today because of wrong motives in their hearts.

Your motives must not only be right in ministry, but also in studying and talking about the ministry entrusted to others. Pray for those in error, but do not gossip or talk negatively about them. They are God's servants to straighten out, not yours.

Esther's motive was not to take the riches and heap them upon herself. Her motive was to be obedient and to respect the king and his palace. As a result, the king favored her above all the women and placed the crown of a queen upon her head. (See Esther 2:17.) Because Esther displayed a humble and correct motive, the favor she received exalted her to a place of position and authority. Her strong character allowed God to strategically place her when the enemy attempted to destroy the Jewish people. Esther was in her place at the correct time.

Fasting and Prayer

Prayer is the power source of a Spirit-filled life. I will not attempt to cover all the benefits of prayer in this book, but I do want to bring out how fasting and prayer prepared Esther to accomplish her task.

Prayer is the vehicle of travel in the spirit. The steering wheel is the Word of God and the fuel is your persistence. There is no wall too thick through which prayer cannot plow. Prayer is vital to your spiritual strength.

In chapters 3 and 4 of Esther, King Ahasuerus had promoted the wicked Haman over all the princes of the region. Haman had a pride problem, and he did not like the fact that Mordecai refused to bow down to him. Once Haman discovered that Mordecai was a Jew, he decided to destroy the entire Jewish nation. The king unknowingly granted his consent, and the decree was published throughout the region. (See Esther 3:5–15.)

Mordecai sent word to Esther, telling her to reveal her Jewish nationality to the king. Esther replied that she had not been summoned by the king in thirty days, and anyone who entered the inner court of the palace would be put to death unless the king raised the golden scepter.

Mordecai responded:

> *Who knoweth whether thou art come to the kingdom for such a time as this?* (Esther 4:14)

God will cause a particular message to rise at a specific time. There will always be certain people who will rise at a certain time to do a certain work. Just as Esther was appointed to arise for one job, so will many be called upon today.

Strong character and a strong spirit will position you to know exactly what you are to do and where you are to go, nothing more or nothing less.

Gideon was a man who had just one job. In Judges 8:23, the people pleaded with him to rule over them and be their king because of his success. But Gideon knew his place, his position, and the season of God. He answered, "I will not rule over you, neither shall my son rule over you: the Lord shall rule over you." Gideon's job was to bring deliverance and help, and he fulfilled it.

Ecclesiastes 3:1 says,

To every thing there is a season, and a time to every purpose under the heaven.

From Mordecai's exhortation, Esther rose up in her spirit and moved to accept her position for the hour. She instructed Mordecai and all of the Jews with him to fast and pray for three days, no food or water. She and her maidens vowed to do the same. (See Esther 4:16.) There is a correct season and a correct time to come forth and do the job you are being positioned to do. Prayer and fasting will keep you alert to God's plan.

To experience the supernatural realm of God, we must be adventurous in prayer. I am sure that Esther and the Jewish nation ventured out on a high level of prayer to receive the understanding that came. Esther received detailed instructions on how to win the favor of the king for the Jewish nation. After the three days of prayer and fasting, Esther invited the king and Haman to dinner. The king graciously accepted and begged her to tell him what she desired of him. Instead of blurting out all she knew, she had built discipline through her godly character and her prayer and fasting and told the king nothing.

She invited the king and Haman back the second night. When they returned, the king's heart was ready to hear all that his queen would ask of him. She explained the dilemma and revealed that Haman had plotted the destruction of the Jews. Because of Esther's courage and timing, not only was Haman hung on the gallows he had prepared for Mordecai, but so were all of his sons, and Mordecai was exalted second only to the king. (See Esther 5:7–8:2.)

Through her strength in God, Esther went all the way. She not only rid her people of the main enemy through Haman, his ten sons were executed as well. (See Esther 9:13.) That is the anointing of those who walk in the timing of God. They will not stop at the first phase of victory—they pursue until the entire problem is conquered.

But the story does not end there. Being accurate in the timing of God produces a harvest of souls. After the victory was proclaimed throughout the region, conviction came to the people.

And many of the people of the land became Jews; for the fear of the Jews fell upon them.   (Esther 8:17)

To this day, the Jewish people celebrate the victory God granted their nation through Esther and Mordecai.

Walking in the correct timing of God produces total victory in every area, every time. The sick are healed, the oppressed go free, the lost are saved—the enemy is defeated, and the kingdom of God progresses!

First Chronicles 12:32 states,

And of the children of Issachar, which were men that had understanding of the times, to know what Israel ought to do.

The word *"understanding"* in the Hebrew means "to perceive."[3] It is the will of God that we perceive by our spirits the time we are

---

3. James Strong, *Hebrew and Chaldee Dictionary*, 20, #995 and #998.

in and then know the job we are to do within that timing. When you are submitted to the time and season God has for you—watch out! You're about to be overwhelmed with the favor of God and man and with abundant blessings from heaven.

6

RECEIVING REMEDY AND RESTORATION

How do you know what God is saying? How can you be sure to be in the correct timing of God? By applying the spiritual principles covered in this book, you can set your heart to hear from God and be in the right place at the right time.

Let me give you some points on how to operate in God's perfect timing.

* *Do not seek another person's opinion as absolute direction on what you sense in your spirit.* Go to the Father in prayer and say, "Father, show me the timing of these things. Help my perception to be stronger."

* *Believe what you get in your spirit.* What you hear in your head can often be wrong, but you will know because you will not have total peace, that peace that passes all understanding. However, believing and following your spirit will always bring total peace.

* *Seek God on the message you hear or read from ministers of the gospel.* A few years ago, I began to feel the anointing for warfare surfacing again in the body of Christ and wrote the book, *The Invading Force.* Many people said, "Boy, he sure is full of youthful zeal and fire." Every time I heard that, my stomach would turn. I knew the message was a word from God delivered in His timing. I knew the attitudes of those people were

a sign of spiritual complacency. They were patronizing God's message and not receiving it. If that message was "youthful zeal," then I want it when I am eighty years old, if the Lord tarries that long. But I heard that comment so often, I began to check myself. I went back to the Lord and prayed, "God, tell me what time it is. Am I preaching what You are doing? Is this a time of war that we are coming into?"

At that time, everyone wanted to hear about love, prosperity, and pleasant things. But down in my spirit, God kept saying to me, "A time of conflict, a time of war has the church come into. This is not a time of peace, but a time of spiritual conflict. You need this anointing for this time." I realized that warfare is always precedence for spiritual harvest.

The best way to check a message or a word is to test it according to the Bible and to pray and ask God about it. Then stay with what you hear in your spirit. Most importantly, make sure the message or word lines up with the Word of God. *Listen to the prophecies you hear.* When those things begin to be fulfilled, you know God's timing is changing.

The Lord said to me once, "When events [such as the walls coming down in Eastern Europe] take place in the last days, they are not to be analyzed, but taken advantage of. My church needs to quit looking and analyzing everything, and instead, see the door that is being opened and go through it."

The events over the past years in Europe and Asia have shown that God will open the windows and doors for the church to reap the harvest before the end comes. Look for the doors of opportunity to preach the gospel of the kingdom.

The church of the last days is to be a church that works. The church will not have time to write books on end-time prophecy as they will be too busy fulfilling those end-time prophecies! We have a duty to "do," not a show to watch. God's clock says to me that revival is in progress and something is about to break open worldwide.

What If You Miss It?

Suppose you do miss the due season. What if, for some reason, you miss the entire timing of something God has for you? Be encouraged! God can redeem the time.

> *See then that ye walk circumspectly, not as fools, but as wise, redeeming the time, because the days are evil.*
>
> (Ephesians 5:15–16)

"Redeeming the time" means to "rescue from loss."⁴ God can recover and redeem the time through His grace and mercy. If you miss it, get up, repent, find out what you did wrong, and go on. Don't dwell on your mistakes and throw yourself one big pity party. Use your mistakes as stepping stones, not stumbling blocks. Even if it seems there may be some things that cannot be recovered, our God is a miracle-working God. All that is required of us is that we trust Him.

How do you get to the place where God will redeem the time? Repent, saying, "Father, I'm sorry for missing it. If You arrange the time for me to do it again, I'll do it Your way. Forgive me for making the mistake. Thank You for redeeming the time for me."

Some of you may be saying, "I was middle-aged or old when I got born again and didn't think there was much I could do. Now I have quit running, and I agree to do what God called me to do." Ask God to redeem the time for you so you can do more in the latter part of your life than you did in the beginning. You can be

4. Strong, *The Exhaustive Concordance of the Bible* (Nashville: Abingdon, 1890), "Greek Dictionary of the New Testament," 29, #1805

that eleventh-hour worker and be a part of a great harvest. (See Matthew 20:1–16.)

I pray this book will help you to better discern the times. Seek God about the seasons in your life, your church, your nation, and your world. I believe you will hear from God, and the separation of the wheat and the tares will find you among the wheat.

ABOUT THE AUTHOR

Roberts Liardon is an author, public speaker, spiritual leader, church historian, and humanitarian. He was called into the ministry at a very young age, preaching his first public sermon at the age of thirteen and lecturing in Christian colleges and universities at age fifteen. At sixteen, Roberts launched a radio program, and at seventeen, he wrote his first book, *I Saw Heaven*, which sold 1.5 million copies. His next book and video series, *God's Generals*, established Roberts as a leading Protestant church historian, and both books brought him international attention.

In his mid-twenties, Roberts built one of the fastest-growing churches in the U.S. and established his first accredited Bible college. From this ministry, he founded more than forty churches, built five international Bible colleges, and assisted the poor and needy in his community, throughout America, and around the globe. Recently, Roberts launched a new TV show called *God's Generals with Roberts Liardon*, which currently airs in more than two hundred nations.

Roberts had the privilege of being mentored by Oral Roberts and Lester Sumrall, and now he is under the covering of both Dr. Che Ahn of Harvest International Ministry and Pastor Colin Dye of Kensington Temple, London, England. As a recognized church historian specializing in the Pentecostal and charismatic movements, he is in demand as a speaker, writer, and mentor. His voice speaks to a current generation of believers who want to draw closer to the heart and mind of God and impact their communities and the nations of the world through the gospel of Jesus Christ.

Roberts Liardon Ministries
P.O. Box 2989 • Sarasota, FL 34230
E-mail: info1@robertsliardon.org • www.RobertsLiardon.com
Twitter: @RobertsLiardon
Facebook: www.facebook.com/RobertsLiardon